The Thinking School

Implementing Thinking Skills Across the School

RALPH PIROZZO

Acknowledgements

The author is grateful to all the teachers that have provided suggestions on how to use the thinking tools presented here, with a special thanks to the following authors for the permission to include their materials in this book: Mark Makepeace for the activities outlined in LEADER (pp. 32-38), Ms Vanessa Hince for the activities relating to scenario 1 in LEAP (p. 40), Kate McGilvray for the activities relating to scenario 2 in LEAP (p. 41), Judy Darby, Diane Gallacher and others who contributed to the development of the STIESA activities (pp. 68-71), to Nicole Crowe for the WASPS activities (pp. 88-93) and finally, to Professor Frank Lyman for his permission to update TPS to TPSS (pp. 106-109).

© 2024 Ralph Pirozzo

This work is copyright. Apart from any pages identified as reproducible and any fair dealings for the purposes of private study, research, criticism or review, or as permitted under the Copyright Act, no part should be reproduced, transmitted, stored, communicated or recorded by any process, without written permission. Any pages identified as reproducible are only authorised for use in the classroom or by any school or nonprofit organisation that has purchased the book. Enquiries should be made to the publisher.

Published in 2024 by Amba Press, Melbourne, Australia.
www.ambapress.com.au

First published in 2013 by Hawker Brownlow Education.
This edition replaces all previous editions.

ISBN: 9781923215085 (pbk)
ISBN: 9781923215092 (ebk)

A catalogue record for this book is available from the National Library of Australia.

Contents

Introduction 1
The Thinking School: Implementing Thinking Skills Across the School 2
A & R (Action and Reaction) 6
ARC (Action, Reaction, Consequences) 6
MAC (My Area of Control) 9-10
BROW (Brainstorm, Review, Organise, Write) 11-12
BROWSE (Brainstorm, Review, Organise, Write, Share, Evaluate) 13
Concept maps 14-17
DMT (Decision Making Tool) 18-19
GLOW (Gather, List, Organise, Write) 20-21
ISACS (Identify, Share, Argue, Compromise, Solve) 22-24
ITPE (Identify, Think, Pair, Explain) 25-27
IW5 (Why, Why, Who, What, What) 28-29
LDC (Like, Dislike, Challenges, Changes) 30-31
LEADER (Listen, Explain, Argue, Debate, Elaborate, Reflect) 32-38
LEAP (Listen, Enjoy, Analyse & Arrange, Perform) 39-41
LIMACE (Locate, Identify, Make, Analyse, Compare and Contrast, Evaluate) 42-43
LITE (Like, Improvements, Timeline, Evaluation) 44-45
MACE (Make, Analyse, Compare and Contrast, Evaluate) 46-48
PSDR (Predict, Share, Do, Reflect) 49-50
RedMast (Read, Estimate, Draw, Make, Arrange, Simplify, Think) 51-54
RIB–TT (Ralph's Inquiry-Based Thinking Tool) 55-58
SCRAM (Substitute, Combine, Rate, Act, Modify) 59-62
SCREAM (Separate, Classify, Rate, Explain, Act, Magnify) 63
SOWC Analysis (Strengths, Opportunities, Weaknesses, Consequences) 64-67
STIESA (Show, Think, Imitate, Explore, Sound, Apply) 68-71
TAP (Think All Possibilities) 72-73
TEAM (Think, Explain, Arrange, Make) 74-76
The Rake 77-79
Thinking clouds 80-81
TREC (Think, Read, Estimate, Calculate) 82-84
Venn diagram 85-87
WASPS (Watch, Ask, Show, Practise, Show) 88-93
WINCE (Want, Identify, Need, Create, Evaluate) 94-95
W chart 96-98
X chart 99-100
Y chart 101-102
Choosing the Right Thinking Tool 103-104
Action Plan for Implementation 105
TPS and TPSS 106-109
References 110

Introduction

Thinking tools are the strategies or scaffolding through which students can access the curriculum. They can be defined as artificial devices that have been developed specifically to improve children's thinking by:

- focusing their attention visually on an issue that needs to be resolved
- offering immediate feedback through seeing their ideas on paper
- seeing the big picture
- making new connections
- analysing complex situations
- explaining relationships between concepts
- developing new thinking skills
- producing a larger number of possible solutions
- making informed choices
- constructing new knowledge
- creating new ideas and products

Thinking tools are not new. In fact, Edward de Bono has been promoting the direct teaching of thinking skills since the seventies through his Cognitive Research Trust (CoRT) and by his pioneering lateral thinking.

What is new and exciting is the fact that the 48- and 56-grid matrix as explained and implemented by Pirozzo (2007, pp. 73–91) provides a framework that enables you to direct students to use the most appropriate thinking tools to solve an issue or a problem. In addition, thinking tools help your students by:

- enabling them to become more engaged in their learning
- assisting them in processing data and information
- providing them with a framework to generate and organise their ideas
- enabling them to transfer their knowledge from Lower Level Thinking Skills (LOTs) to Higher Level Thinking Skills (HOTs). LOTs refer to the Knowing, Understanding and Applying thinking levels of Bloom's Taxonomy, whereas HOTs refer to the higher levels of analysing, creating and evaluating

Thinking tools should be hyperlinked and/or embedded into the matrix so that students can use them on interactive whiteboards in order to increase their engagement level.

All thinking tools that appear in this book are available as one downloadable PDF via the password-protected internet portal. Visit **go.hbe.com.au**, select *The Thinking School* from the list of titles and enter the password provided in the imprint page of this book.

The Thinking School: implementing thinking skills across the school

It is essential that thinking skills are implemented school – wide in a clear manner of scope and sequence as part of a thinking skills program. This program should be a public document so that every teacher, student and parent becomes fully aware of the five new thinking tools that will be introduced every year (in both primary and secondary schools). Furthermore, this program will set out the thinking tools that will need to be revised at the beginning of each year. This will be particularly important to students who are new to the school and to those who may have missed a good deal of schooling due to illness or travelling interstate and overseas.

Below is an example of a whole – school thinking skills program that has been implemented in a primary school. Each of the thinking tools listed in this program shall be addressed in more detail within this book.

P-6 Thinking Tools

P-1	Year 2	Year 3	Year 4	Year 5	Year 6
LDC	Review P-1 Thinking Tools and introduce the following tools:	Review P-2 Thinking Tools and introduce the following tools:	Review P-3 Thinking Tools and introduce the following tools:	Review P-4 Thinking Tools and introduce the following tools:	Review P-5 Thinking Tools and introduce the following tools:
TEAM					
Y CHART					
X CHART	LITE	ARC	IW^5	ITPE	DMT
W CHART	A & R	MAC	PSDR	LEAP	ISACS
STIESA	GLOW	BROW	Trec	WASPS	BROWSE
TPS &TPSS	RIB-TT	MACE	WINCE	LEADER	LIMACE
Concept Maps	The Rake	SCRAM	SCREAM	RedMast	SOWC analysis
Thinking Clouds					

For example, a Year 2 teacher at this school will be expected to introduce the LITE, A & R, GLOW, RIB – TT and the Rake thinking tools to their students, and review the ten P – 1 thinking tools that the students should already be familiar with.

It is important to note that in relation to this school's thinking skills program, LITE, A & R, GLOW, RIB – TT and the Rake represent the minimum number of thinking tools to be introduced in Year 2. More tools can be introduced at the teacher's discretion.

While working in primary education, it is very advantageous to implement thinking skills across the whole school. However, this approach has not worked well in secondary education. In secondary schools, teachers prefer to implement thinking skills at the faculty level. For example, the English faculty may decide to introduce the following Year 7–12 thinking skills program:

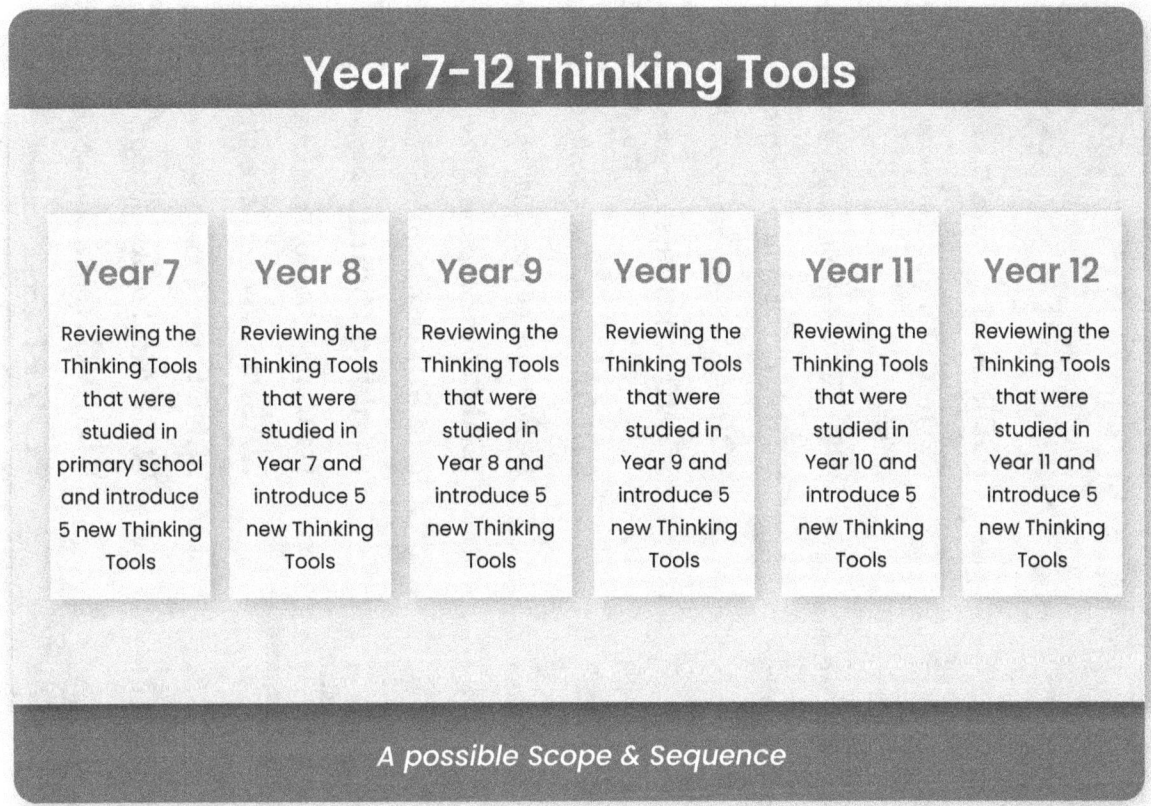

A possible Scope & Sequence

What are the benefits of implementing thinking skills either at the school – wide level in primary education or at the faculty level in secondary schools?

By doing this every teacher, student and parent will know what is expected at each year level. This means that every year, students will:

- have the opportunity to review the tools that were introduced in the previous year(s)
- be introduced to a minimum of five new thinking tools

From the teacher's point of view, this is advantageous because they will choose the thinking tools to be introduced and will know exactly what is expected of them. In other words, everyone will be speaking the same language. This "scope and sequence" approach to the implementation of thinking skills will ensure that teachers at the same year level (primary) or faculty (secondary) are using the same thinking tools.

Thinking Toolkit

A & R: *Action and Reaction*

ARC: *Action, Reaction and Consequences*

BROW: *Brainstorm, Read, Organise, Write*

BROWSE: *Brainstorm, Read, Organise, Write, Share, Evaluate*

Concept Maps: *A convergent thinking tool organiser*

DMT: *Decision Making Tool*

GLOW: *Gather, List, Organise, Write*

ISACS: *Identify, Share, Argue, Compromise, Solve*

ITPE: *Identify, Think, Pair, Explain*

IW^5: *Why, Why, Who, What, What*

LDC: *Like, Dislike, Challenging/Changes*

LEADER: *Listen, Explain, Argue, Perform*

LEAP: *Listen, Enjoy, Analyse & Arrange, Create, Evaluate*

LIMACE: *Locate, Identify, Make, Analyse, Create, Evaluate*

LITE: *Like, Improvements, Time line, Evaluation*

MAC: *My Area of Control*

MACE: *Magnify, Act, Classify, Empathise*

PSDR: *Predict, Share, Do, Reflect*

RedMast: *Read, Estimate, Draw, Make, Arrange, Simplify, Think*

RIB–TT: *Ralph's Inquiry-Based Thinking Tool*

SCRAM: *Substitute, Create, Rewrite, Audition, Modify*

SCREAM: *Separate, Classify, Rate, Explain, Act, Magnify*

SOWC Analysis: *Strengths, Opportunities, Weakness & Consequences*

STIESA: *Show, Think, Imitate, Explore, Sound, Apply*

TAP: *Think All Possibilities*

TEAM: *Think, Explain, Arrange, Make*

The Rake: *Touch, Smell, Taste, Look, Listen, Think*

Thinking Clouds: *A divergent thinking tool organiser*

Trec: *Think, Read, Estimate, Calculate*

WASPS: *E=Watch, Ask, Show, Practise, Show*

WINCE: *Want, Identify, Need, Create, Evaluate*

W CHART: *Looks, Sounds, Feels, Tastes, Thinks*

X CHART: *Looks, Sounds, Feels, Thinks*

Y CHART: *Looks, Sounds, Feels,*

Given the fact that schools are incredibly busy places and teachers have little spare time, how can this be achieved?

The author has implemented thinking skills school – wide in primary schools and at individual faculty level in secondary schools by encouraging every teacher to build his or her own thinking toolkit containing a minimum of 25 thinking tools.

Given the fact that there are so many thinking tools available, which should be included in a teacher's thinking toolkit?

Teachers will select the thinking tools that they believe will provide the most effective and efficient way of enhancing their students' ability to think and to learn.

At the earliest opportunity, the school or faculty should form a committee with responsibility for reviewing the current selection of thinking tools created by a variety of authors and educators. It is essential for this committee to review the work of a number of authors rather than aligning themselves with only one or two to ensure that they do not limit themselves and inevitably limit their students' learning potential.

Another major function of the committee is to present a variety of thinking tools to all staff. A very useful strategy that has been employed by many schools is to set aside ten minutes during regular staff meetings so that a member of the committee can introduce one thinking tool at a time. The teachers are then encouraged to use this particular thinking tool and report back on whether or not it has worked in their classroom at the next staff meeting. This process is then repeated until each teacher has selected a minimum of 25 tools. These will then make up the individual teacher's thinking toolkit.

The figure overleaf shows the author's present thinking toolkit, including definitions of each acronym used.

How can these thinking tools be used to "scaffold" children's learning?

The author will now provide ways of using these thinking tools. However, his expectation is that teachers will experiment with these tools in their own classrooms in order to find many more exciting and challenging ways of using them. In doing so, teachers will provide the most engaging learning environment for all students. Enjoy the journey!

A & R, ARC and MAC

Action and Reaction
Action, Reaction, Consequences
My Area of Control

A & R Strategy

ACTION	REACTION
What will you do now?	How will the other person react?

The A & R Strategy is best suited to younger children

Description

The A & R and the ARC are thinking tools that will help children to empathise with other people and make informed decisions.

Scenario 1

In completing an integrated project entitled "Out in Space" (Pirozzo, 2007, pp. 80–83) the children need to build a space station with a workforce made up of:

- a manager
- a doctor and a dentist
- a nurse
- two supervisors
- 40 workers

A & R, ARC and MAC (Action, Reaction, Consequences)

A great deal of time, energy and money has been spent in ensuring that all the individuals chosen work well together. However, it's hard to imagine that there will be no conflict when a large number of individuals are asked to work together in such a restricted environment.

Using their interpersonal and visual intelligences, students could use the A & R and ARC to solve the following conflicts:

1. While an experienced worker is completing a job on the space station, the supervisor comes over and yells, 'What are you doing? Can't you see that this is completely wrong?' How should the worker reply to the supervisor? Use A & R to frame your answer.

2. After just two weeks on the space station, one of the workers finds that he/she doesn't share any of the team's values, interests or hobbies and has lost all interest in the project. Role play this scenario by working through the three stages involved in the ARC. The aim of this activity is to show the worker that for any action taken there will be a reaction from the other team members, their supervisors and the manager. Undeniably, there will also be consequences.

A & R, ARC and MAC can be used to deal with issues relating to teasing, bullying and discipline problems.

Scenario 2

Felicity, a Year 7 student at a large metropolitan secondary school, sits by herself in an isolated area of the playground during morning and lunch breaks. Julie, a Year 9 student, regularly teases her. The playground teacher overhears Julie saying, "No one likes you because you've got freckles and you are just too fat and ugly." The teacher sees Felicity drop her head and sob uncontrollably. The teacher approaches Julie and counsels her: "You should not be teasing Felicity because this is not fair. This sort of behaviour will not be tolerated at this school. How would you feel if other students were to call you names?" Julie abruptly replies, "Everyone picks on me at this school and you know that I was only joking. I didn't mean to hurt anyone."

At this stage, we can use A & R to deconstruct the scene.

Action (A)	Reaction (R)
Julie believes that teasing Felicity is acceptable behaviour and that nothing will happen to her because she is just "joking".	Felicity sobs uncontrollably and is obviously very upset.

Usually, after being spoken to, one would expect that the student would stop the offending behaviour and thus no further action would be needed. Unfortunately, in this case, Julie's teasing escalates to spreading rumours about Felicity's sexuality through emails, SMS and social networking sites. The teacher realises that the situation has deteriorated significantly and refers Julie to the Head of Department. Based on the school's behaviour policy, the

Head of Department determines that this is no longer "teasing" but is in fact bullying and decides to use ARC to deal with the situation.

Action (A)	Reaction (R)	Consequences (C)
Julie's teasing has escalated to bullying Felicity through emails, SMS and social networking sites.	Felicity has further withdrawn from the rest of the students, feels insecure, vulnerable and worthless, and feels that no – one likes her. On a number of occasions, she has been heard saying, "Life is just not worth living."	The Head of Department advises Julie that a letter will be sent home, she will be kept in for detention after school for the next five days and she is expected to write a letter apologising to Felicity.

The Head of Department had hoped that Julie's behaviour would change after this, but unfortunately she now begins stalking Felicity at school and on her way to and from home. The Head of Department decides that the matter should be referred to the Principal, who quickly contacts Julie's parents and informs them that unless she immediately stops spreading the offending rumours, removes the material posted on social networking sites and stops stalking Felicity, the police will be called in and Julie will be expelled.

Julie's parents can't believe that their daughter could have done anything like this and that obviously Julie has been completely misunderstood. They point out that Julie is well liked by all her friends and that she would never hurt anyone. Furthermore, they emphasise that they do not want their daughter to be at a school that treats students like they are criminals, and does not allow students to express themselves. They argue that the phone call from the Principal was the last straw. They decide to move Julie to a much more democratic school.

Once Julie has left the school, the Head of Department and the Principal encourage Felicity to complete MAC (My Area of Control). In completing MAC, Felicity learns that although there are certain issues that are beyond her control, there are other issues that are within her area of control.

MAC: My Area of Control

Things that you cannot change are:

Things that you can change are:
-
-
-
-
-
-
-

I will try ---------------------------- ⎫
I can try ----------------------------   ⎬ What will I try first?
I am try ----------------------------   ⎭

This thinking tool is specifically designed to enable children to deal with various issues.

Things beyond Felicity's control	Things that Felicity can control
- Felicity cannot force Julie to like her. - Felicity cannot stop Julie from attending the same school. - Felicity cannot decide what actions the school will take against Julie. - Felicity cannot decide whether or not Julie's parents enrol her at a different school.	- Felicity does not have to sit by herself during morning and lunch breaks in an isolated area of the playground. Felicity can: - report teasing, bullying and stalking to teachers, Heads of Department, the Deputy Principal and the Principal - play games with other children during breaks - ask the playground teacher for help - spend time in the library during breaks - volunteer to spend some of her breaks working with younger children

Reflection

- In small groups, discuss different strategies that could have been used to resolve this issue.
- Apart from A & R, ARC and MAC, what other thinking tools could have been used?

BROW

Brainstorm, Review, Organise, Write

How to get the most out of BROW?

Brainstorm (B)	Read (R)	Organise (O)	Write (W)
The following visual organisers will be of great help to you in brainstorming: 1. Concept Maps 2. Thinking clouds 3. KWL 4. TAP	1. Read the material 2. Do you understand what you are reading? 3. Use the dictionary or the internet to find out the meaning of a particular word. 4. Please do not hesitate to ask other students and/or your teacher for assistance.	These five visual organisers will assist you greatly in "seeing" a particular issue from another person's point of view: 1. X chart 2. Y chart 3. W chart 4. The Rake 5. Venn diagram	Now, use all the information available to you to commence writing your report or story. An excellent strategy is to break your work into small "chunks". Once you have written your first draft, then ask your teacher for her/his comments.

Description

In using BROW, the children go through a four – stage process:

1. **B**rainstorming
2. **R**eading and reviewing the relevant material
3. **O**rganising the information
4. **W**riting a report or story

Scenario

You have been chosen to design a marketing campaign for a new boat. You will need to prepare a single page advertisement for the boat. The advertisement may be for a newspaper, magazine or website.

1. Brainstorm all the different techniques that are used in advertising using thinking tools such as concept maps (pp. 14 – 17), thinking clouds (pp. 80 – 81) or TAP (Thinking All Possibilities, pp. 72 – 73).

2. Read and review other advertisements for new products. Add to your list the important things these advertisements mention and the techniques used.

3. Organise your information. Use pictures and words for your own advertisement. Use a variety of visual organisers to help you such as W, X and Y charts (pp. 96 – 102) and the Rake (pp. 77 – 79).

4. Write the first draft of your advertisement.

The use of W, X and Y charts and the Rake has been found to be extremely useful in "guiding" children into writing. Undeniably, in addition to these, there are many more thinking tools that should also be considered in this "scaffolding".

Pirozzo (2007, pp. 90–91) has a complete case study on the use of scaffolding tools, with the "Marketing your boat" activity.

BROWSE (Brainstorm, Review, Organise, Write, Share, Evaluate)

BROWSE

Brainstorm, Review, Organise, Write, Share, Evaluate

BROWSE

Brainstorm — B

The following thinking tools will be of great help to you in brainstorming:

1. Concept maps
2. Thinking clouds
3. KWL
4. TAP

Read — R

1. Read the material
2. Do you understand what you are reading?
3. Use a dictionary or the internet to find out the meaning of a particular word.
4. Please do not hesitate to ask other students and/or your teacher for assistance

Organise — O

These five thinking tools will assist you greatly in deconstructing and comparing a character(s) and to organise your ideas/thoughts:

1. X chart
2. Y chart
3. W chart
4. The Rake
5. Venn diagram

Write — W

Now, use all the information available to you to write the first draft of your report/story.

An excellent strategy is to break your work into small "chunks".

Read your first draft a number of times to make sure that it makes sense and it reads well.

Share — S

Once you have written your first draft, then share it with your teacher/group/class. Use either TPS or TPSS as useful cooperative learning strategies.

Evaluate — E

The first draft usually needs to be improved. Thus evaluate it by:

1. Yourself
2. Your peers
3. Your teacher

Use the LDC to get feedback and then, based on the comments or suggestions received, prepare your final report/story and hand it in for assessment.

Description

BROW can be updated to BROWSE to enable students to:

1. share their work with other children and their teachers
2. evaluate what they have created in order to further improve their products

Concept Maps

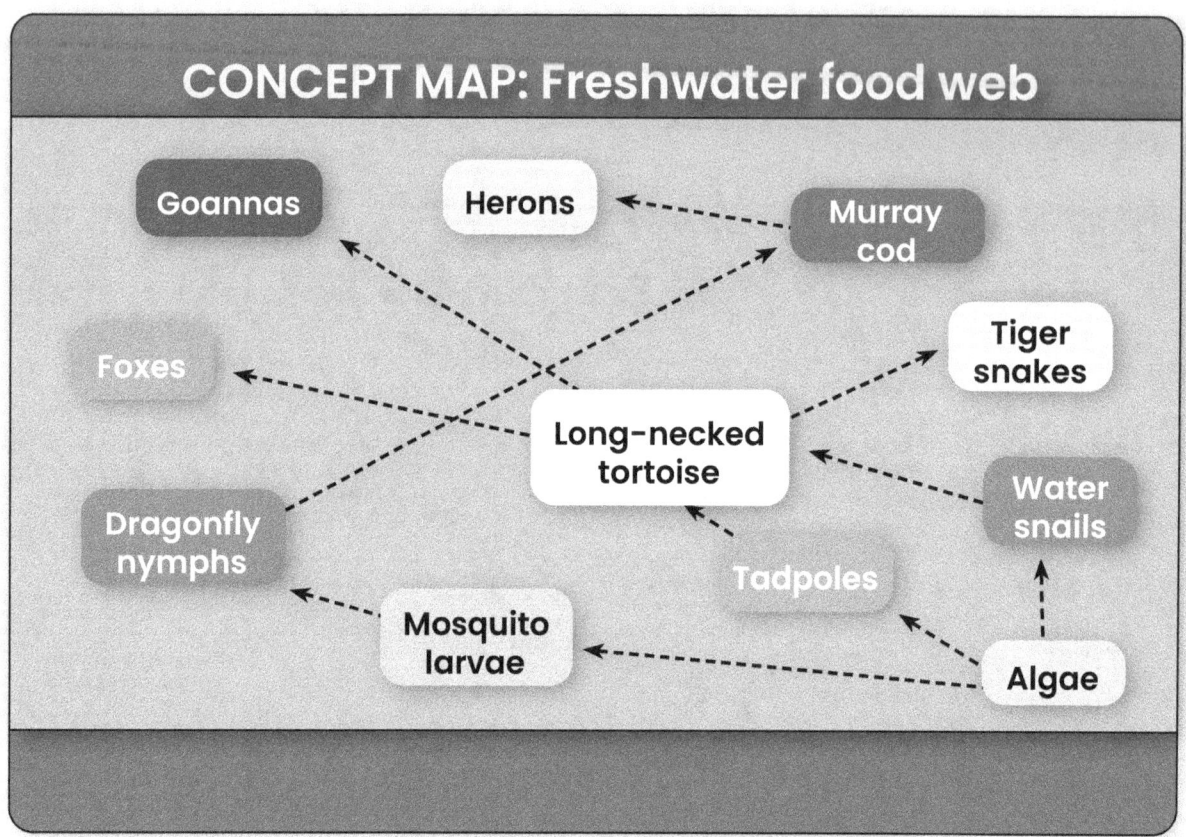

Description

Concept maps are extremely useful in enabling students to see the "big picture" and to organise data by discovering relationships between various components. Because concept maps lead the brain to begin in one area and then proceed through a logical and sequential framework, they tend to favour convergent learners.

Scenario

Create you own food web.

1. Cut out each food web card (these can be found on the next page).

2. Organise each of them in a way that makes sense to you, thinking about what each creature eats.

3. Glue the food web cards onto butcher's paper.

Concept Maps

4. Connect each creature with a straight line in order to show what it eats.

5. Draw an arrow at the end of each line to indicate that this creature eats the insect, plant or animal at the other end of the line.

6. Write "eaten by" on each line.

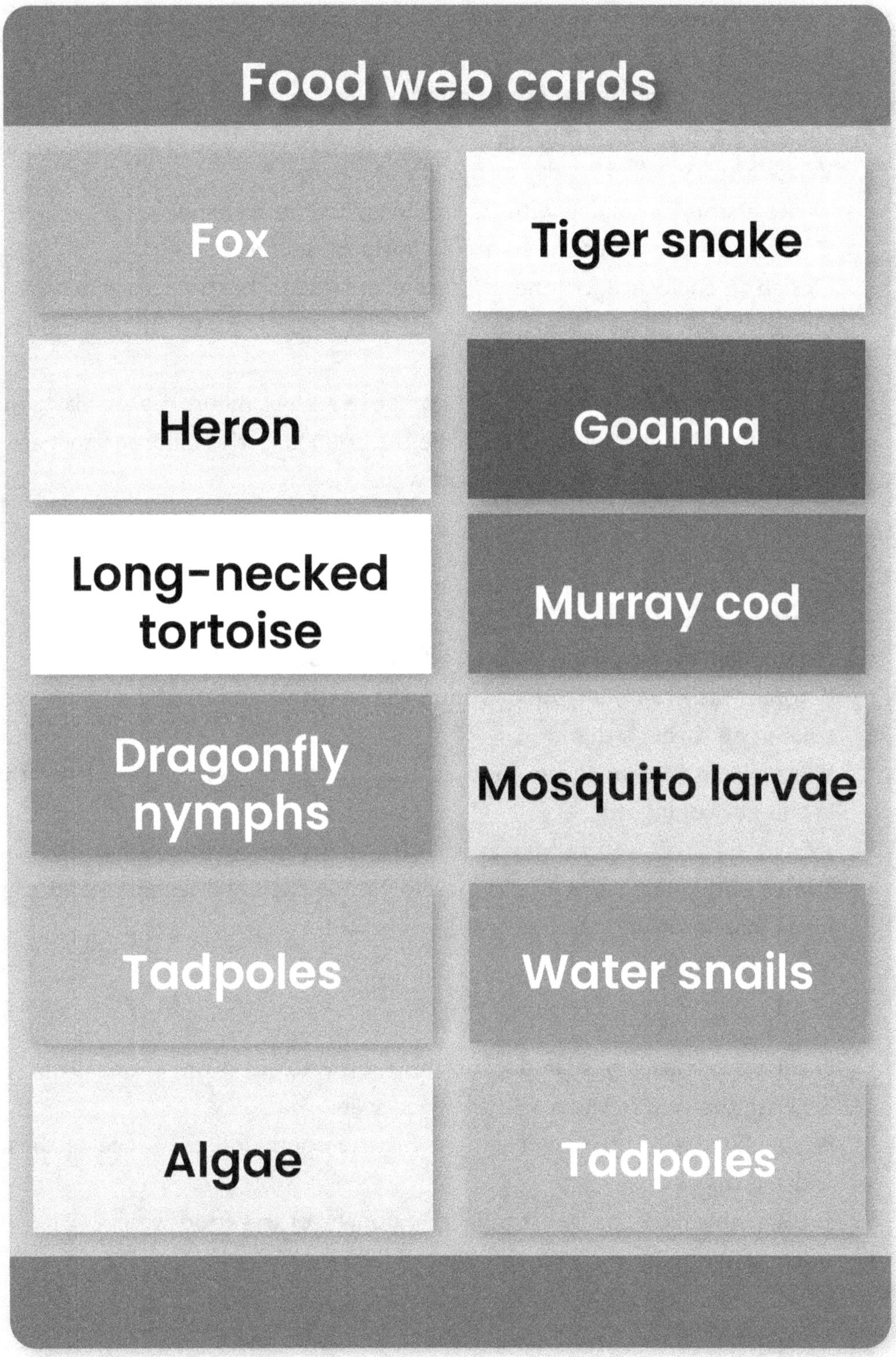

Food web cards

- Fox
- Heron
- Long-necked tortoise
- Dragonfly nymphs
- Tadpoles
- Algae
- Tiger snake
- Goanna
- Murray cod
- Mosquito larvae
- Water snails
- Tadpoles

Extension activities

Create

- Create a diorama of the environment where these organisms live.
- Create an energy pyramid for this food web.
- Create a Dreamtime legend based on this food web.
- Draw pictures to show how the creatures interact.
- Design an environmental board game.
- Choreograph a dance relating to this food web.
- Write a story called "A day in the life of a heron".
- Write a story beginning with "On the way to the water hole …"
- Create a poster about the harmful effects of pollution.
- Design an enclosure for one of these creatures to become your pet.
- Design a new insect, plant or animal that could survive in this food web and explain how it fits in.
- Choose one of the creatures and compose a song, mime, rap or play about it.
- Use percussion instruments to make the sounds of the different animals.
- Find pictures to include in the food web.

Discuss

- What do algae eat?
- How would an introduced animal affect this food web?
- If toxic waste was introduced into the wetland environment, how would the toxins rise through the food web?
- What would happen to the food web if a farmer sprayed herbicide on the plants in this environment?
- Would this food web survive as it is? Is there anything missing?
- Which of the organisms would survive if the billabong dries up due to drought or man's interference?

Analyse and research

- Predict the impact of pollution on this food web.
- Evaluate the role of the fox in the food web.
- Recommend a healthy environment for the continued existence of these plants and animals.
- Explain why algae are an essential component of this food web.
- Investigate how foxes were introduced into Australia.

Classify and compare

- Use colour coding to show water, land and flying insects, plants or animals.
- Classify the organisms into groups.
- Separate all the organisms into herbivores, carnivores and omnivores.
- Select one land organism and one water organism and use a Venn diagram to compare them.

Act

- Role play the various animals in the food web.
- Choose an animal from the food web and act it out in front of the class. The rest of the class guess which animal you have chosen.
- Interview a fisherman whose livelihood depends on the Murray cod.
- Write and perform a play about this food web.

Reflection

Concept maps tend to converge, thus focusing and producing a single solution. They achieve this by harnessing the energy that is created by thinking clouds (a divergent thinking tool, pp. 80 – 81). Whenever possible, teachers should use thinking clouds and concept maps simultaneously in order for their students to develop effective and efficient problem – solving techniques.

DMT

How do you make critical decisions regarding controversial and sensitive issues such as:

- Adoption laws
- Building desalination plants
- Building new dams
- Building nuclear plants to produce electricity
- Child labour
- Drilling for oil under the Great Barrier Reef
- Drinking recycled water
- Gay marriages
- Global warming
- Greenhouse gas emissions
- How to deal with refugees?
- How to deal with those responsible for the collapse of HIH, Westpoint Corporation Pty Ltd and One:Tel
- Laws that prevent individuals from placing offensive material on the internet
- Lowering or increasing the drinking age
- Reconciliation issues
- Stem cell research
- Uranium mining
- Which political party to join?
- Which political party to vote for?
- World hunger
- World poverty

The decision making tool may assist you in deciding where you stand on some of these issues.

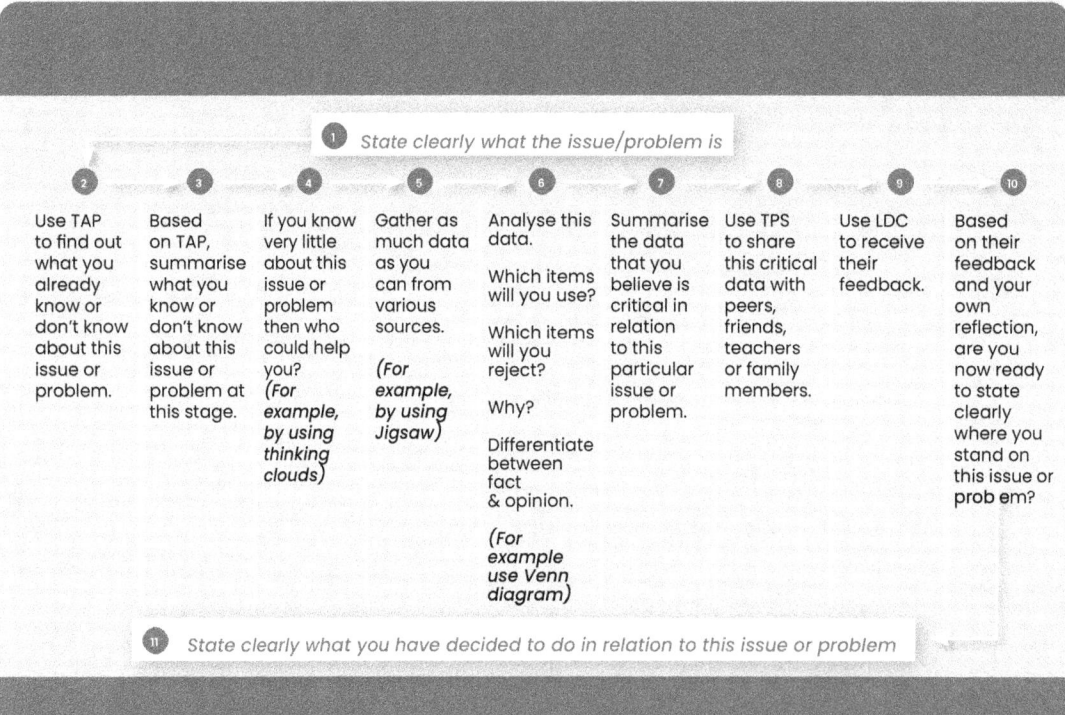

1 State clearly what the issue/problem is

2 Use TAP to find out what you already know or don't know about this issue or problem.

3 Based on TAP, summarise what you know or don't know about this issue or problem at this stage.

4 If you know very little about this issue or problem then who could help you? *(For example, by using thinking clouds)*

5 Gather as much data as you can from various sources. *(For example, by using Jigsaw)*

6 Analyse this data. Which items will you use? Which items will you reject? Why? Differentiate between fact & opinion. *(For example use Venn diagram)*

7 Summarise the data that you believe is critical in relation to this particular issue or problem.

8 Use TPS to share this critical data with peers, friends, teachers or family members.

9 Use LDC to receive their feedback.

10 Based on their feedback and your own reflection, are you now ready to state clearly where you stand on this issue or problem?

11 State clearly what you have decided to do in relation to this issue or problem

DMT (Decision Making Tool)

Description

DMT is a decision – making tool that has been designed specifically to assist students to make critical decisions regarding controversial and sensitive issues such as adoption laws, global warming and stem cell research. DMT takes the students through 11 steps, commencing with stating clearly what the issue or problem is, and finishing with stating clearly what decision has been made in relation to this issue or problem.

Scenario

Teachers can choose any of the 21 different scenarios that are listed in the DMT. If necessary, they can also add their own topics. Regardless of the topic chosen, it is important that the students go through the 11 critical steps as indicated.

The Thinking School: Implementing Thinking Skills Across the School

GLOW

Gather, List, Organise, Write

Gather	List	Organise	Write
• Gather all the relevant information (using the Internet or books)	• List the information that will be most useful to you	• Sort, select, omit, add • and layout • Sequence ideas • Subheading • Sentence structure • Paragraph formation • Use X, Y, W charts & the Rake to generate and elaborate ideas	• Write your first draft and then share it with your peers and your teacher for their feedback

A possible learning sequence that students can use to write their first draft

Description

GLOW provides children with four simple steps that can be used to write the first draft of a story or report.

1. **G**ather the information.

2. **L**ist the most useful information.

3. **O**rganise the information.

4. **W**rite your first draft.

Scenario

Children are asked to prepare the first draft of a report entitled: "How can we stop global warming?" By using GLOW, the children will carry out the following steps.

GLOW (Gather, List, Organise, Write)

1. Gather

This is the information – gathering stage when children read books, encyclopedias, newspapers, magazines and search the Internet to find as much information as possible relating to global warming.

2. List

The children will categorise this material into three folders:

1. Must use
1. Could use
2. Of no use

At first, they will focus their attention on the material collected in the "Must use" folder and only return to the "Could use" folder later on, if more information is required. Listing the information that will be most useful to them is a critical stage.

3. Organise

This involves the children paying attention to the following:

- prioritise information
- sort, select, omit and add information
- layout
- presentation
- scaffolds
- sequence ideas
- headings and subheadings
- sentence structure
- paragraph formation
- meta – language
- criteria – based rubrics
- use W, X and Y charts (pp. 96 – 102), the Rake (p.p 77 – 79), TAP (p. 72) and Venn diagrams (pp. 85 – 87) to generate ideas

4. Write

The children are now ready to write the first draft of their report. Once written, the children will share it with their peers, in groups, with the whole class and/or with their teacher in order to receive feedback based on the LDC (like, dislike, challenge, pp. 30 – 31) and/or LITE (like, improvements, timeline, evaluation, pp. 44 – 45) thinking tools.

ISACS
Identify, Share, Argue, Compromise, Solve

ISACS

Identify

Share

Argue

Compromise

Solve

ISACS (Identity, Share, Argue, Compromise, Solve)

Description

ISACS provides the students with five clear steps with which to solve issues that impact directly on their lives.

Scenario

The children are attending a school located in a large metropolitan city where space is very limited. The Principal has reported that a large number of girls are no longer participating in any sporting activities and has invited the Student Council and the teachers to come up with a plan of action. The Student Council and the teachers have decided to use ISACS as their preferred thinking tool in the hope that they will resolve this problem.

1. Identify

The issue to be resolved is "Why are a large number of girls no longer participating in any sporting activities?"

2. Share

Using TPS (Think, pair, share) and/or TPSS (Think, pair, share, square) (pp. 106 – 109), share with your pair or group why a large number of girls are no longer participating in any sporting activities. Write all the comments on a large piece of butcher's paper or the whiteboard.

3. Argue, debate, discuss

The comments gathered during the share stage are now discussed as a whole group. It has become clear from the comments gathered that:

- both boys and girls need to be involved in sporting activities
- due to very limited space, the boys are preventing the girls from participating in any sport by being "pushy" and "rough"

4. Compromise

Suggestions for how to solve this problem are now gathered with the aim of reaching a compromise. A number of suggestions have been put forward including:

- given the fact that the boys are being "pushy" and "rough", all sporting activities should be stopped for both boys and girls

- girls have missed out on so much time in the playground that from now on the boys should be prevented from participating in any sporting activity
- the school has two small areas available for sport, thus it has been suggested that one of these areas should become "Boys only" and the other should become "Girls only"

5. Solve

The solution agreed upon during the compromise stage is now implemented. In the latest newsletter, the Principal reports that the school will be setting up one of the playgrounds as a "Boys only" area and the other as a "Girls only" area.

Reflection

The following questions can be used to reflect on this scenario:

- Do you think that this solution will work? Why or why not?
- Do you think there are more effective ways of dealing with this issue? Is so, list them.
- Which thinking tool did you find most useful for this brainstorming activity?

ITPE
Identify, Think, Pair, Explain

ITPE

Identify

Think

Pair

Explain

Description

ITPE has been devised specifically to help children and teachers deal with issues relating to safety. It can be used in areas as diverse as science, design and technology, woodwork, metalwork, food technology, hospitality, agricultural science and other practical subjects.

Scenario

A science teacher is welcoming the Year 7 students to the chemistry laboratory for the first time and has chosen to use ITPE in the hope that this tool will encourage the students to use the chemicals and equipment in a safe manner. This may take more than one period to achieve.

1. Identify

The teacher shows the children how to use the following chemicals and equipment safely and identifies relevant safety issues when using:

- Bunsen burners
- test tubes
- wooden tongs
- acids
- bases
- tripods
- fume hood

The teacher also uses various posters to identify safety issues that the students must follow while in the laboratory.

2. Think

The teacher asks the students to think about safety issues such as:

- What will happen if you touch the Bunsen burner whilst the gas is on?
- What will happen if you point a test tube to the face or eyes of another student while a chemical reaction is taking place?
- What will happen if you do not use wooden tongs to hold a test tube that is hot?
- Why should you never run in the laboratory?
- Why should children with long hair tie their hair back in the chemistry lab?
- What should you do in the event of a spill?

ITPE (Identify, Think, Pair, Explain)

3. Pair

The teacher now uses TPS (Think, pair, share) and/or TPSS (Think, pair, share, square) (pp. 106 – 109) to pair the students.

4. Explain

The students now explain to their partner or group why rules in the laboratory are extremely important. They demonstrate how to use the Bunsen burner, test tubes, wooden tongs, acids, bases and other pieces of scientific equipment in the safest possible way.

Once the students have demonstrated that they can use various chemicals and equipment safely, they will be given certificates and/or licences to use specific equipment such as the Bunsen burner.

IW⁵

Why, Why, Who, What, What

IW⁵				
Why	**Why**	**Who**	**What**	**What**
do I want this?	does it have to be this specific brand?	am I trying to compete with?	am I prepared to do to get this?	other items am I prepared to buy instead of this?

Description

Are students' self images being shaped by peer pressure, advertising and the need to consume? IW⁵ takes the students through five stages to assist them in value clarification, social skills, budgeting and independent choice making. These steps are:

1. Why do I want this?
2. Why does it have to be this specific brand?
3. Who am I trying to compete with?
4. What am I prepared to do to get this?
5. What other items am I prepared to buy instead of this?

Scenario

A teacher explores with a group of Year 6 students the impact of peer pressure, advertising and the media in shaping their self – image and the products that they buy by using IW⁵.

IW⁵ (Why, Why, Who, What, What)

1. Why do I want this?

Use thinking clouds (pp. 80 – 81) to discover the goods that students would like to have and then separate these goods into "Needs" versus "Wants" on a Venn diagram. Ask the students to choose the best advertisement that they have seen recently and apply either the W, X or Y chart (pp. 96 – 102) or the Rake (pp. 77 – 79) to discover how skilful advertising people are at convincing students that they have to buy certain goods. If possible, source some advertisements that bombard the students with messages such as "You are worth it", "You deserve it" and "Want it all and want it now".

2. Why does it have to be this specific brand?

Ask the students why they need to have specific brands of mobile phones, shoes, mp3 players etc. Students discover that most of the time they want a particular brand because they desperately want to be seen as cool and as belonging to a particular group. Thus, often the material goods that they crave have a lot to do with their need to belong.

3. Who am I trying to compete with?

By brainstorming, the students discover that they want to compete with the coolest kids in the classroom, with those students who appear to them to be leaders, risk takers and those who constantly challenge figures of authority.

4. What am I prepared to do to get this?

We often hear students saying, "I would do anything to get the latest label!" Some students are prepared to get part – time jobs to save enough money to buy these items. Other children pressure their parents into purchasing these very expensive items.

5. What other items am I prepared to buy instead of this?

Often, the answer is "nothing else will do!"

Reflection

- Have the students clearly identified what constitutes a "need" and what constitutes a "want"?
- What do students mean when they say "I wouldn't be caught dead wearing that brand"?
- Do students believe that advertising has a major impact on the material goods that they crave and eventually buy? If so, what is the role of parents and teachers?

LDC
Like, Dislike, Challenges, Changes

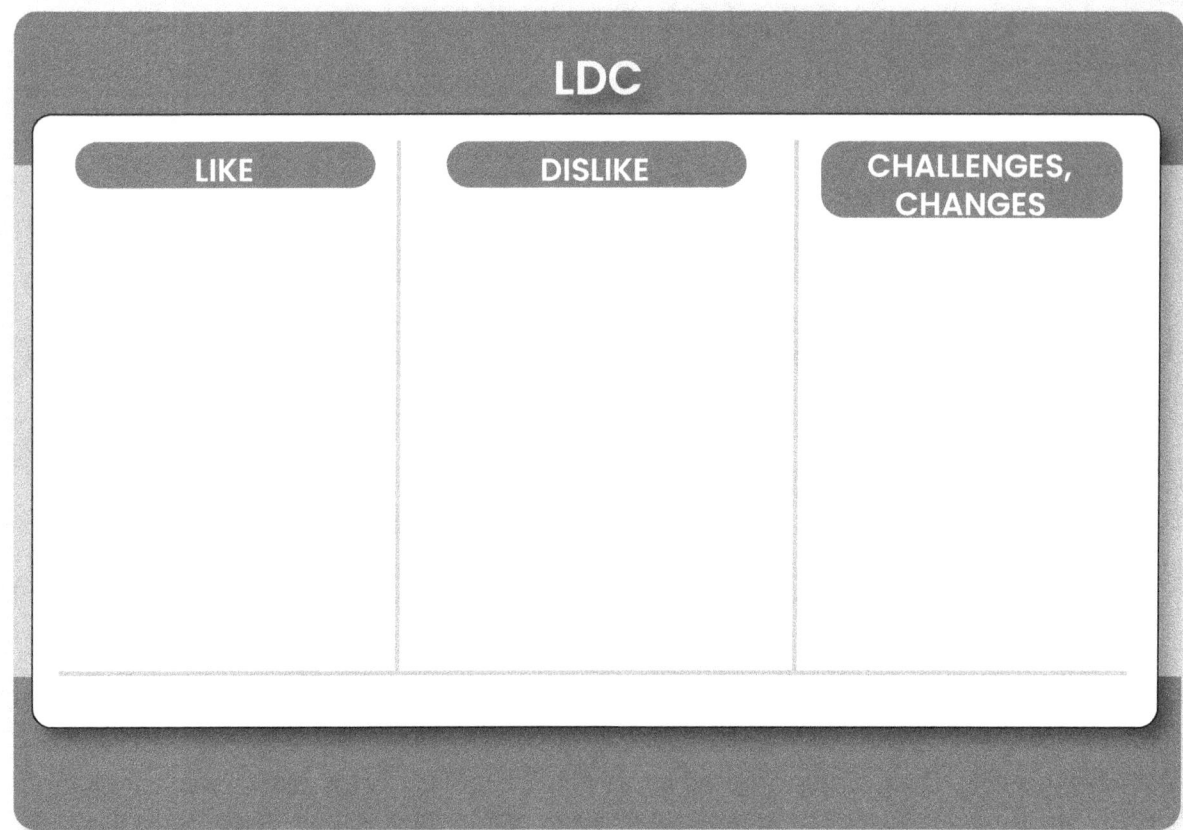

Description

The LDC is a reflective thinking tool that can be used in three different ways: (1) self – assessment; (2) teacher assessment; and (3) peer assessment. This tool encourages students to reflect on their work and to receive feedback from their teachers and peers in a safe and structured manner.

L represents the good things about an idea or a thing.

D signifies the negative aspects.

C refers to aspects that are challenging or that can be modified.

Teachers can use the LDC to provide feedback to their students in a variety of situations including:

- teacher – student
- teacher – groups of students
- teacher – entire class

The LDC can also be used by students to provide feedback to other students based on the relevant rubric. It can also be used for self – reflection.

Scenario

Prepare a poster of a plant – eating dinosaur and present your work to the class. Now, invite the other students to provide feedback by using the LDC.

I like …

I dislike …

I found … challenging.

These are the changes you should make …

LEADER

Listen, Explain, Argue, Debate, Elaborate, Reflect

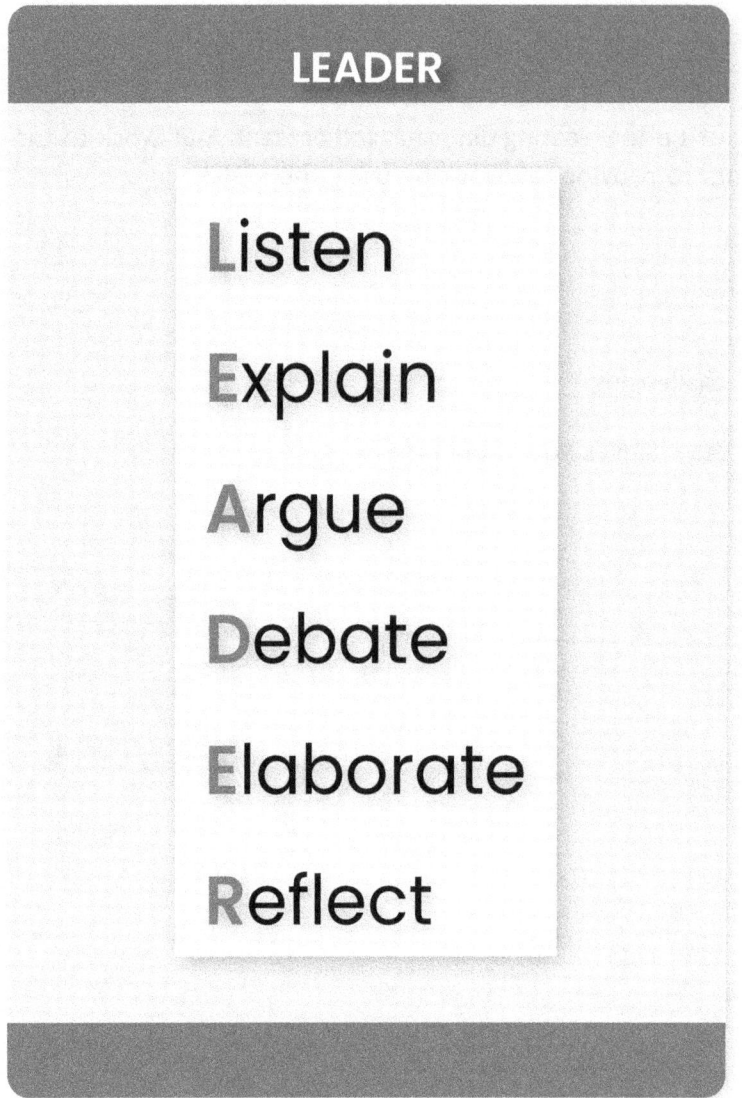

Description

LEADER prepares children for a debate by taking them through the six steps listed above. The strength of LEADER is the scaffolding that it provides for a team preparing for a debate., and as such, LEADER is best utilised in the specific teaching of how to develop a debate. Since it is structured and explicit, it is very useful for debaters of all levels of experience.

LEADER (Listen, Explain, Argue, Debate, Elaborate, Reflect)

Scenario

The teacher organises a debate on one of the following topics:

- Mobile phones should be banned from the classroom.
- Boys should have more space to play sport than girls.
- Students should face regular mandatory drug tests.
- Students should be able to vote when they are 16 years old.
- There should be a curfew for people under the age of 16 in order to reduce crime.
- Farming of chickens in cages should become illegal.
- Cosmetic companies should continue using animals to test their products.
- All countries should implement a carbon tax.
- Adopted children have the right to know who their biological parents are.
- Whaling should be allowed.
- The Olympic games are a waste of money.
- Advertising of tobacco products should be allowed.
- Companies that produce alcohol should sponsor local sporting teams.
- Logging should be allowed in national parks.
- Mining and oil exploration should be allowed in the Arctic and Antarctic.
- Nuclear power plants should be built in every big city.
- Euthanasia should be legalised.
- Recreational drugs should be decriminalised.
- The making of body parts using gene therapy should become a legitimate business.
- Students should wear a school uniform.
- Students should pray at the beginning of each school day.

Students are divided into teams. When a team is working together to prepare their "case", LEADER becomes an invaluable tool because the students will need to do the following.

1. Listen

Team members listen to each other's ideas. Each team member is given the opportunity to contribute to the discussion. Arguments to support their team's case are collated. At this time, the team members could also begin to consider the case of their opposition, allowing them to anticipate their arguments and be prepared for their rebuttal. They could brainstorm by using thinking clouds.

2. Explain

Team members explain what their ideas are about and why they are worthy of consideration. The explain stage takes place at the same time as the listen stage.

3. Argue

The team works together to organise the arguments that they will put forward. They need to allocate each point to a speaker. Ideally the arguments should be split along a theme, for example:

- how the argument affects the individual
- how the argument affects the wider community or society
- the general or "big picture" view
- a specific view
- the environmental reasons
- the practical reasons
- the moral reasons
- the economic reasons

Some of the points can be allocated to the first speaker, whose primary purpose is to define the debate topic and to support the path that his or her argument will take. The majority of the points need to be given to the second speaker as they have the most time to develop the argument. No points are to be allocated to the third speaker as their primary role is to summarise their team's argument.

The team should also work together to look at what arguments the opposing team could put forward. This allows the team to have rebuttal prepared for the opposing team. All speakers in a debate, except for the first speaker for the affirmative, have to rebut. Rebuttal should follow this basic structure:

- what was said
- who (which speaker) said it
- why it is wrong

For example:

The first speaker for the affirmative said that, "According to the opponents, mobile phones should be banned in classrooms due to potential radiation poisoning. We in the negative believe this to be incorrect because there has not been a conclusive study published that has definitively shown that mobile phone usage increases risks of radiation poisoning."

4. Debate

The team members debate their topic, taking into account possible rebuttal. This is when the speakers begin to write their debate. They look at the tasks that they have to fulfil as a particular speaker (1st affirmative, 1st negative, 2nd affirmative, etc.) The teacher should designate a set amount of time for each speaker, and the team members need to be aware of this when writing their debate.

LEADER (Listen, Explain, Argue, Debate, Elaborate, Reflect)

5. Elaborate

The team members elaborate on their arguments. Each individual begins to "flesh out" the ideas that they have been allocated. They need to gather factual evidence to support their ideas, not hearsay and/or personal opinions. All sources that are used (the Internet, research papers, newspaper reports etc.) need to be referenced.

6. Reflect

The team members reflect on what they have prepared both individually and as a team, and fine – tune any areas of concern. The team members present their debate to each other for a number of reasons:

- to check that they are under the allowed time (leaving room for rebuttal)
- to check that all ideas that were agreed upon have been covered
- to allow each member the opportunity to listen to and provide feedback to each speaker

A support person (a teacher or a coach) could be a part of this last step.

Improving listening skills prior to the debate

Given the fact that some children have poor listening skills, the teacher or coach can use the following methods to improve listening skills prior to the debate.

1. Describing pictures

For this activity, one child (the "describer") is given a piece of paper with a picture on it. This picture is not of any particular object, but should be strange, involving lots of shapes, letters and numbers, and should be hidden from all children apart from the describer. The describer then has to describe the picture to the rest of the class, who try to draw the same picture by following the instructions given. When the description is finished, the child who most accurately reproduced the picture becomes the describer and is given a new picture to describe to the class.

2. Bingo

This is another useful game for improving children's listening skills.

The debating process

1. Chairperson

During the debate, one child can be appointed as chairperson. The chairperson's role is to explain to all participants the rules of the debate. The chairperson:

- sits between two teams
- welcomes all participants
- calls the debate to order
- announces the topic of the debate
- names the adjudicators, the timekeeper and the participating teams

2. Timekeeper

One child should be appointed timekeeper. The timekeeper's role is to ensure that each speaker keeps within the designated amount of time.

3. Adjudicators

Two or more children can be appointed as adjudicators during the debate. The role of the adjudicators is to judge the debate based on the following marking scheme:

- Matter (40 marks): Was the speech logical and relevant?
- Manner (40 marks): Was the speech persuasive? Did the speaker use his or her voice, palm cards, gestures, eye contact, stance and humour to the best of his or her ability?
- Method (20 marks): How well did the speaker construct and organise his or her speech?

4. The first affirmative speaker must:

- define the topic
- present the line taken by the affirmative team
- outline briefly what each speaker in their team will talk about
- present the first half of the affirmative case.

5. The first negative speaker must:

- accept or reject the first affirmative speaker's definition
- present the negative team's line
- outline briefly what each of the negative speakers will say
- argue and/or rebut a few of the main points of the affirmative team

LEADER (Listen, Explain, Argue, Debate, Elaborate, Reflect)

6. The second affirmative must:
   - reaffirm the affirmatives team's line by presenting the second half of their case
   - rebut some of the main points of the negative team

7. The second negative speaker must:
   - rebut the affirmative team's main points (about one – third of the allocated time should be spent on this)
   - present the second half of the negative team's case

8. The third affirmative speaker must:
   - reaffirm the affirmative team's line
   - rebut all the remaining points of the negative team
   - present a summary of the affirmative team's case
   - round off the debate for the affirmative team

9. The third negative speaker must:
   - reaffirm the negative team's line
   - rebut all the remaining points of the affirmative team
   - present a summary of the negative team's case
   - round off the debate for the negative team

10. At the conclusion of the debate, the adjudicators should:
    - be given time to prepare their feedback and decide which team won the debate
    - be positive and constructive
    - rate each speech using the marking scheme provided in step 3
    - point out mistakes and provide suggestions for improvement
    - explain clearly why the successful team won the debate

Reflection on feedback

Based on the adjudicators' feedback, how can you improve your debating skills? Consider their feedback in terms of matter, manner and method.

Matter

Was your speech logical and relevant?

Manner

Was your speech persuasive? Did you use your voice, palm cards, gestures, eye contact, stance and humour to the best of your ability?

Method

How well did you construct and organise your speech?

The author is grateful to Mr Mark Makepeace for his permission to include the activities outlined in the LEADER in this book.

LEAP
Listen, Enjoy, Analyse & Arrange, Perform

L isten

E njoy

A nalyse & arrange

P erform

Description

LEAP provides the teacher with four steps that can be used to teach many music topics and concepts in a logical progression. These steps are:

1. **L**isten to the song or piece of music.

2. **E**njoy the song or piece of music.

3. **A**nalyse, arrange, or rearrange the song or piece of music.

4. **P**erform the song or piece of music.

Scenario 1

A teacher wants her primary school students to create their own rhythmic ostinatos to accompany a song and has chosen LEAP as her preferred thinking tool.

1. Listen

As a first step, the teacher plays the chosen song and the students listen.

2. Enjoy

The students are allowed to tap or groove along with the song as long as they are not disturbing the other students.

3. Analyse, arrange, rearrange

The students try out various different rhythms with the song and pick the one that they like the most. At this stage, the teacher encourages the class to share their ideas. The students then try out the various rhythms that have been suggested. Next, the students vote to select the rhythm that they feel best accompanies the song. The teacher now discusses with the students which instruments they should use to play the rhythm and allows time for practice.

4. Perform

Working in small groups, the students perform their own ostinato for the rest of the class and use TPS to reflect on their work. As a follow – up activity, the students should write their own ostinatos, select the relevant instruments and perform to the class.

Scenario 2

A secondary school music teacher uses LEAP with her students to analyse music.

1. Listen

Give students a new piece of music to study. Let them hear it first. They should have the score of music in front of them, so they are able to follow the score as they hear the music.

2. Enjoy

The students are allowed to play or sing along with the recording. The students have the opportunity to work out key components of the song, such as riffs, chord patterns and melodic patterns.

3. Analyse, arrange, rearrange

The students analyse the score, looking for repetition and other music concepts such as the key signature, time signature, speed, different rhythms used and dynamics. Then, the students discuss the structure of the music and what changes could be made to it. In the HSC exam, the focus is on making the piece "yours" and so the students should talk about the changes that could be made to the structure, dynamics, texture, instrumentation and even the key of the piece.

4. Perform

The students perform the piece of music and look at concepts that they may have missed.

The author is grateful to Ms Vanessa Hince and Ms Kate McGilvray for their permission to include the LEAP activities outlined in scenario 1 & 2 respectively in this book.

LIMACE

Locate, Identify, Make, Analyse, Compare and Contrast, Evaluate

LIMACE

L	I	m	A	C	E
L abel	I dentify	M agnify	A ct	C lassify	E mpathise
L ink	I llustrate	M ake	A dvise	C ompare	E mpower
L iquefy	I magine	M atch	A nalyse	C omplete	E stimate
L iquidate	I mitate	M ime	A pply	C ompose	E valuate
L ist	I nterview	M inimise	A rgue	C onduct	E xperiment
L isten	I mpersonate	M odify	A rrange	C onstruct	E xplain
L ocate	I mprove		A ssess	C ontrast	E xpress
L odge	I nclude		A udition	C reate	E xtrapolate
L ook	I nterpret				
	I nterview				

A possible sequence that students can use to improve their level of creativity

Description

LIMACE is a versatile thinking tool because different verbs can be selected from each of the six columns depending on the activity that the students are involved in.

Scenario

The teacher wants the students to build a bridge of their own choosing in order to discover that triangular shapes provide the most strength of any other shape. The students work in groups of four and each group is provided with:

- 150 plastic straws
- a glue gun loaded with glue (ensure the glue gun is only operated by an adult)
- two blocks of wood (20 cm x 20 cm)
- masking tape
- a book weighing 500 grams

LIMACE (Locate, Identify, Make, Analyse, Compare and Contrast, Evaluate)

The aim of this activity is for each team to build the most inexpensive bridge (1.5 metres tall by 1 metre wide) that will hold a book weighing 500 grams. Each team will be given two hours to build their bridge. The cost of the materials and labour will be charged as follows:

- plastic straws = 5 cents each
- roll of masking tape = $2.50 each
- block of wood = $1.50 each
- hiring of glue gun = $1.00 per hour
- labour = $5.00 per hour/per person

1. Locate

Locate pictures of different types of bridges by searching the internet, various books, encyclopedias and magazines.

2. Identify

Identify which type of bridge you will build. Draw a plan for the bridge, then explain to your group why you have chosen this type of bridge. Then, as a group, decide whose bridge design best fits the criteria.

3. Make

Working as a group, make your chosen bridge using the materials provided. Split into two groups, with each pair commencing their half bridge from opposite starting points. The two pairs should meet halfway in order to link the bridge. Think carefully about how you can strengthen the bridge so that it will hold the weight of the book.

4. Assess, advise

Once you have built your bridge, you are ready to test its strength by placing a book weighing 500 grams on top of it. Is your bridge able to support this book? If not, then advise how you can improve the design of your bridge so that it will hold the book. Then, calculate how much your bridge cost to build using the prices stated above.

5. Compare and contrast

Use a Venn diagram to compare and contrast your bridge with other groups' bridges. Compare the bridges that held the book with those that were not able to do so. How did the successful groups strengthen their bridges? Which shape provides the most strength?

6. Evaluate

Choose the winner of this bridge building competition by evaluating the bridges in terms of strength and cost. Investigate how to reduce the costs of building your bridge and how to improve its strength. In addition, evaluate why triangular shapes are the strongest shapes.

LITE

Like, Improvements, Timeline, Evaluation

LITE

Like	Improvements	Timeline	Evaluation
These are the things that I like about your:	These are the things that need to be improved:	The student is now ready to devise a timeline in which they will improve their:	The student presents their:
1. _____	1. _____		_____
2. _____	2. _____	_____	to the teacher for final evaluation, assessment or marking
3. _____	3. _____	(as indicated by teacher)	
4. _____	4. _____		
(Teacher/student)	(Teacher/student)	(Student)	(Teacher/student)

A possible sequence that teachers can use to provide feedback to their students

Description

LDC was updated to LITE in 2010 to provide students with a four – stage process for giving and receiving feedback. LITE is a reflective thinking tool that can be used in three different ways: (1) self – assessment; (2) teacher assessment; and (3) peer assessment. This tool encourages students to reflect on their work and to receive feedback from their teachers and peers in a safe and structured manner.

L represents the good things about an idea or a thing.
I represents the improvements that need to be made.
T refers to a timeline for the required improvements to be carried out.
E refers to presentation of students' work for evaluation by the teacher.

LITE (Like, Improvements, Timeline, Evaulation)

Teachers can use LITE to provide feedback to their students in a variety of situations including:

- teacher–student
- teacher–groups of students
- teacher–entire class

LITE can also be used by students to provide feedback to other students based on the relevant rubric. It can also be used for self – reflection.

Scenario

A Year 8 teacher has set the following assessment task: "How can we prevent the koala from becoming extinct?" The students need to create their own action plan which will be presented to various groups including students, teachers, administrators, parents, local government officials and a number of environmental groups. The teacher has chosen LITE to provide feedback to students throughout the planning process. It can also be used during the final presentation.

1. Like

The teacher peruses the students' work and states four things that they like about each action plan.

2. Improvements

The teacher reviews each action plan and suggests four alterations that should be made in order to improve the plan.

3. Timeline

Students establish a timeline for making the suggested improvements to their plan.

4. Evaluation

Students present the final copy of their action plan to the teacher for evaluation. In addition, teachers will further evaluate the final presentation of the action plan and determine each student's final mark.

NB: A rubric will be used at every stage of LITE.

MACE

Make, Analyse, Compare and Contrast, Evaluate

MACE

M	A	C	E
M agnify	**A** ct	**C** lassify	**E** mpathise
M ake	**A** dvise	**C** ompare	**E** mpower
M atch	**A** nalyse	**C** omplete	**E** stimate
M ime	**A** pply	**C** ompose	**E** valuate
M inimise	**A** rgue	**C** onduct	**E** xperiment
M odify	**A** rrange	**C** ontrast	**E** xplain
	A ssess	**C** onstruct	**E** xpress
	A udition	**C** reate	**E** xtrapolate

A possible sequence that students can use to improve their level of creativity

Description

MACE is a versatile thinking tool because different verbs can be selected from each of the four columns depending on the activity that the students are involved in.

Scenario

A Year 5 geography teacher wants the students to discover how to prevent soil erosion. The students work in groups of four and each group is provided with:

- two cardboard boxes
- a pair of scissors
- sticky tape
- a ruler
- a bucket of topsoil
- a bucket of grass clippings or hay
- paper or plastic cups
- two bowls

MACE (Make, Analyse, Compare and Contrast, Evaluate)

1. Make

Using the cardboard boxes provided, the students complete the following steps.

- Make two identical boxes with the following dimensions: Length 25 cm x Width 25 cm x Depth 5 cm.
- Label one "box A" and the other "box B".
- Fill box A with topsoil only.
- Fill box B with the same amount of topsoil used in box A. Then, add a layer of grass clippings or hay on top of the soil. Gently pack the grass clippings or hay.
- Place both boxes on a slight slant of about 15 degrees and gently pour the same amount of water, using a cup measuring about 200 ml, onto the top of each box.
- Collect the run – off from box A and box B in two separate, equally – sized bowls.

2. Analyse

The students reflect on the following questions to analyse their results.

- Which bowl has the most amount of water in it? Why? Explain fully.
- Which bowl has the most amount of topsoil in it? Why? Explain fully.

3. Compare and Contrast

- Use a Venn diagram to compare and contrast the results from box A and box B. What is the only difference between box A and box B?
- Research the term "variable" and explain what it means to your group or class.
- What was the variable in this experiment?
- Look at the picture below. Are your results similar? Explain why or why not.

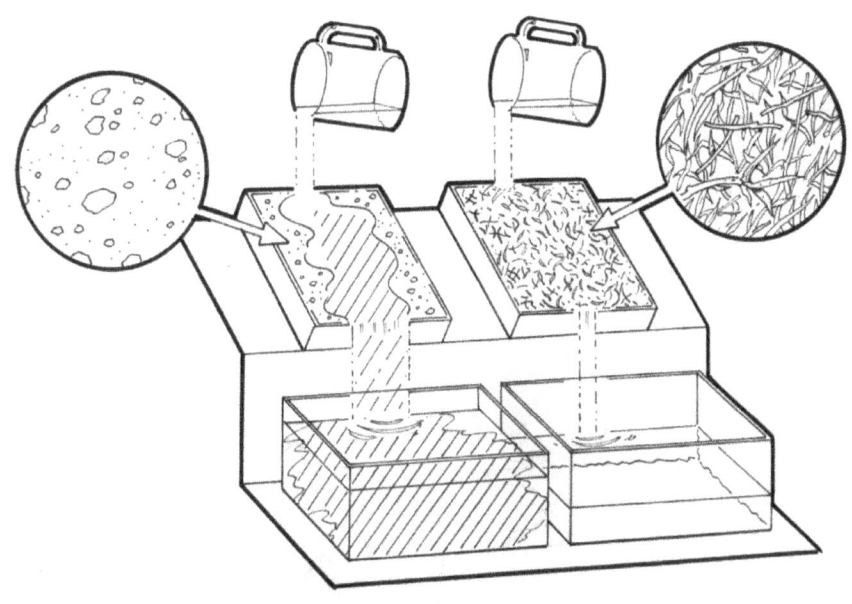

4. Evaluate

The students evaluate their results and suggest improvements that could be made.

- Suggest ways that this experiment could be improved for more reliable results.
- Why are variables important?
- How can you ensure that other students will be able to duplicate your results?

Reflection

1. Based on what you have learned in this experiment, advise the following individuals what they should do to prevent soil erosion:

- a developer who is going to chop 25 acres of land, which is presently covered with native grasses and trees, in order to build 100 house lots

- a homeowner who has moved into a brand new house and finds that the builder has removed the topsoil from the garden, leaving it bare

- a farmer who is planning to harvest their wheat crop and then plough the fields. Given the fact that the farmer knows that a major storm is predicted to hit the area in the following week, what should the farmer do?

- a mining company that is extracting iron ore and coal from the ground.

2. Advise the government which laws should be passed at the local, state and national level to prevent topsoil from being washed into creeks, rivers, lakes and oceans.

PSDR

Predict, Share, Do, Reflect

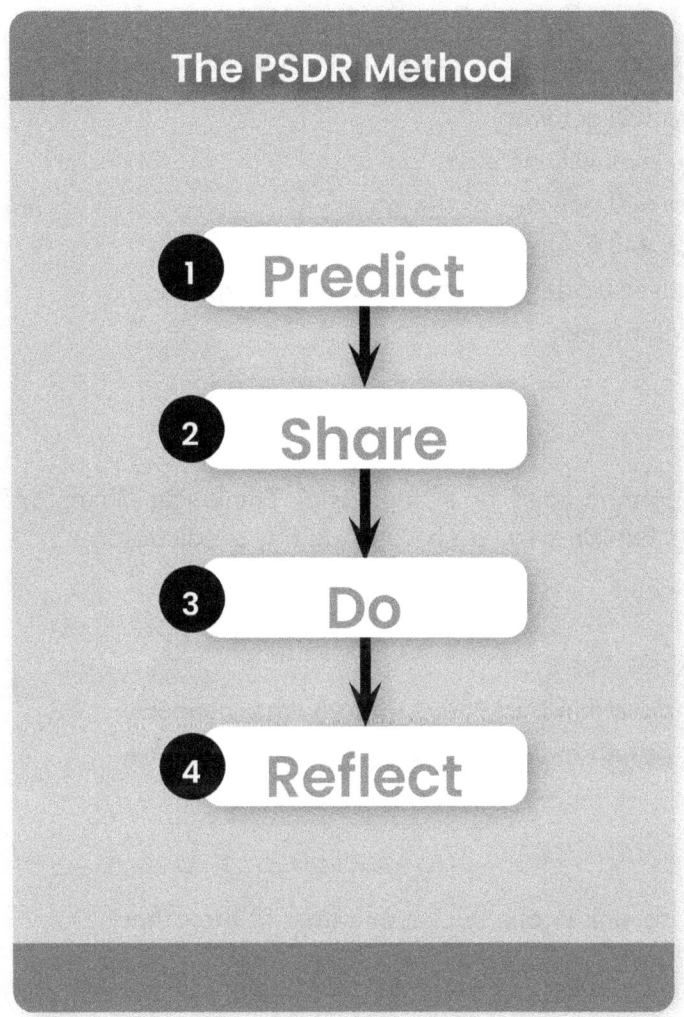

Description

The PSDR method encourages students to go through a four – stage thinking process that involves:

1. **P**redicting the outcome of an experiment

2. **S**haring their predictions with others

3. **D**oing the experiment

4. **R**eflecting on the outcome of the experiment

Scenario

Prepare two similar buckets as follows:

- bucket A: 3.5 litres of boiling water and 200 grams of salt
- bucket B: 3.5 litres of boiling water and 800 grams of salt

1. Predict the outcome of the experiment

What will happen when a potato is placed in each bucket? Suggestions may include:

- the potato will get wet
- the water level will increase
- the potato will pop out of the water
- the potato will float or sink
- water will get inside the potato and it will explode
- nothing will happen

2. Share your predictions

Share your predictions in pairs or groups using Think–Pair–Share or Think–Pair–Share–Square (p. 106-109). Explain why you have made this prediction.

3. Do the experiment

- Place the potato in bucket A. Observe what happens.
- Place the potato in bucket B. Observe what happens.

4. Reflect

Why does the potato sink in one bucket and float in the other?

If the experiment fails, invite your students to modify the relevant variables in order for the potatoes to:

- sink in bucket A
- float in bucket B

Since the density of the water has been altered a great deal by adding 800 grams of salt to bucket B, this is the reason why the potato floats in this bucket. In modifying the variables, we have added an M (Modify) to the original PSDR and thus it now becomes PSDRM (Predict, Share, Do, Reflect, Modify).

RedMast (Read, Estimate, Draw, Make, Arrange, Simplify, Think)

RedMast
Read, Estimate, Draw, Make, Arrange, Simplify, Think

RedMast: Use words, pictures and numbers to solve maths problems

- **READ** — Do you understand the question?
- **ESTIMATE** — Estimate the value of C
  - A = 4cm
  - B = 3cm
  - C = ?
- **DRAW** — Now, calculate the perimeter. Draw a diagram
- **MAKE** — Make a table
- **ARRANGE** — Arrange a list
- **SIMPLIFY** — Make it simpler
- **THINK ABOUT** — Use your reasoning skills

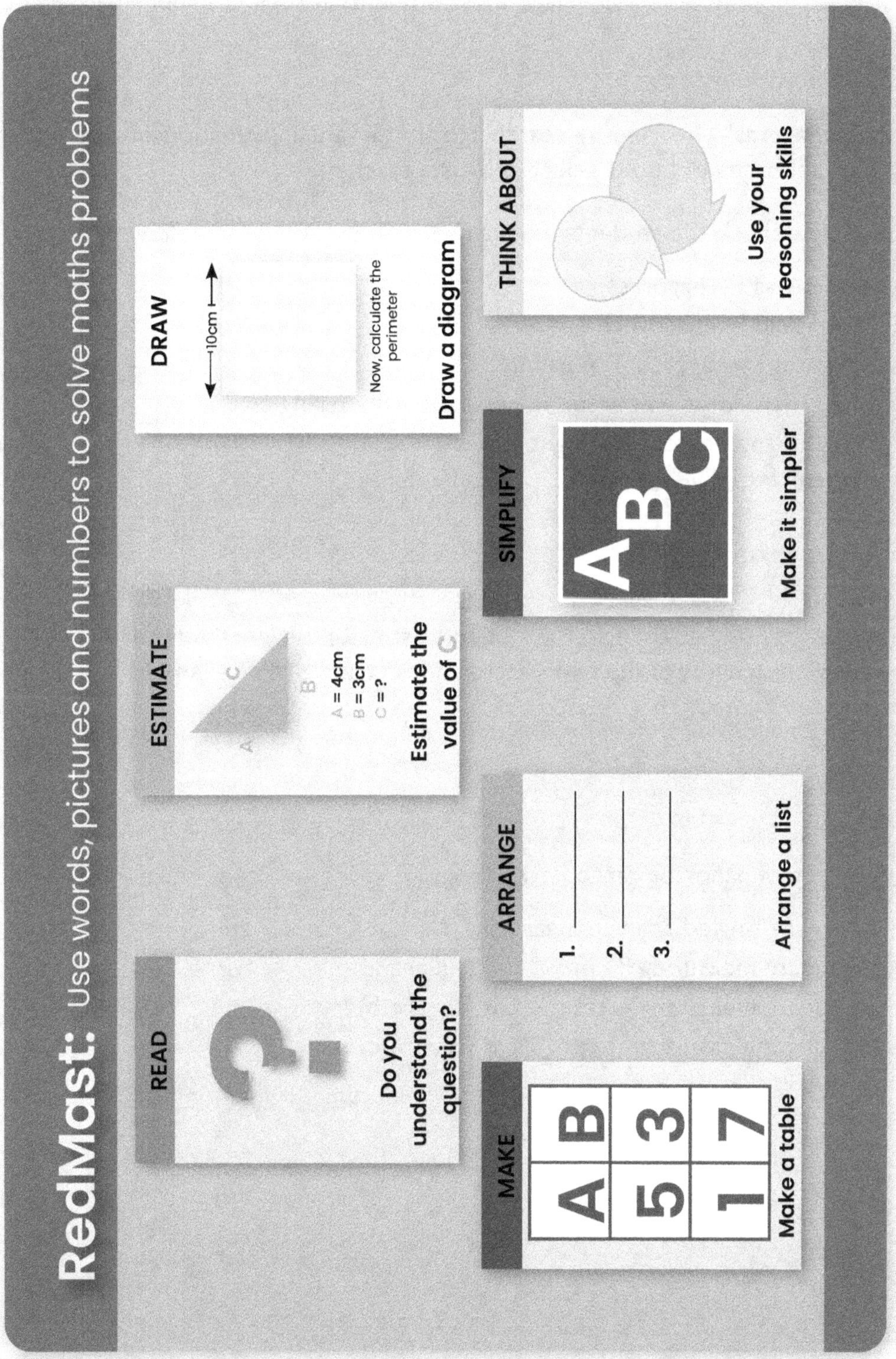

Description

RedMast helps students to solve maths problems by using words, pictures and numbers.

Scenario

A secondary maths teacher has discovered that a number of Year 9 students are having problems understanding and applying Pythagoras' Theorem. The teacher decides to use RedMast in the hope that it will engage these students through multiple learning pathways.

1. Read

Research Pythagoras' Theorem by searching for relevant information on the internet and reading relevant pages of books selected by the teacher.

After this stage, check the students' comprehension by asking the following questions:

- Who was Pythagoras?
- What did he discover?
- What is Pythagoras' Theorem?
- Can Pythagoras' Theorem be applied to any triangle?
- How many degrees is a right angle?
- What is the hypotenuse of a triangle?

2. Estimate

Looking at a right – angled triangle, the students estimate the length of the long side (c) when they are given the lengths of the two shorter sides (a and b). For example: Estimate the value of c if a = 3 cm and b = 4 cm.

3. Draw

On an A3 piece of paper or cardboard, draw:

- a right – angled triangle measuring 3 cm x 4 cm x 5 cm
- a square measuring 3 cm x 3 cm (square a)
- a square measuring 4 cm x 4 cm (square b)
- a square measuring 5 cm x 5 cm (square c)

RedMast (Read, Estimate, Draw, Make, Arrange, Simplify, Think)

4. Make

Now cut out the four shapes that you have drawn. Using a pencil, draw equidistant lines to divide each square into identical tiles (1 cm x 1 cm) as follows:

- divide square a (3 cm x 3 cm) into nine identical tiles
- divide square b (4 cm x 4 cm) into 16 identical tiles
- divide square c (5 cm x 5 cm) into 25 identical tiles

Label each side of the right – angled triangle as follows:

a = 3 cm

b = 4 cm

c = 5 cm

5. Arrange

Arrange the triangle and the three squares that you have cut out. Place the triangle in the middle and place:

- square a next to side a of the triangle
- square b next to side b of the triangle
- square c next to side c of the triangle

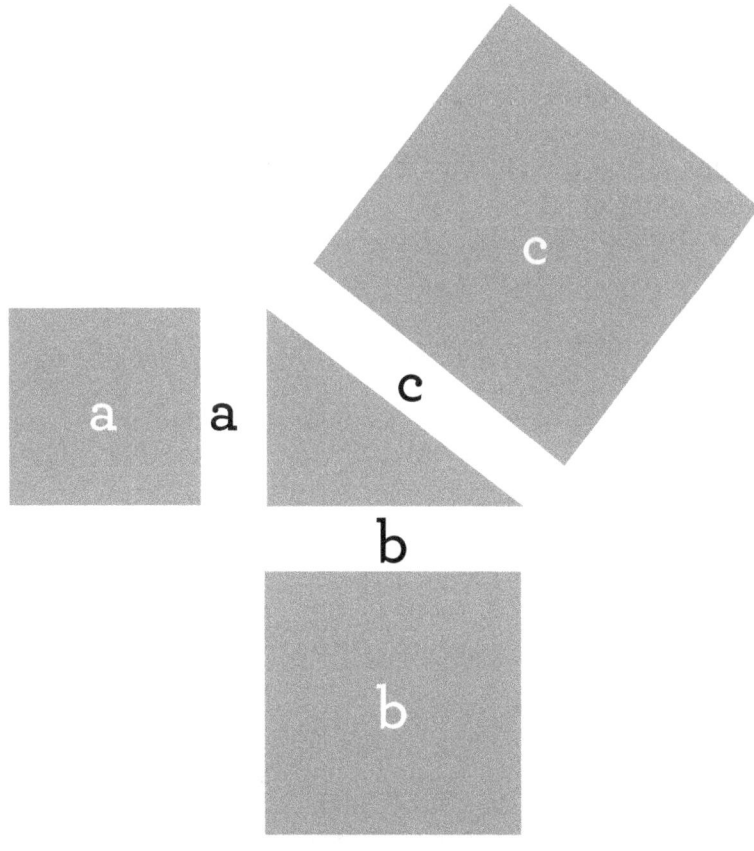

6. Simplify

If Pythagoras' Theorem is correct, then the area of square c must be the same as the areas of squares a and b put together. To find the area of each square, simply count the number of tiles.

- How many tiles are in square a?
- How many tiles are in square b?
- How many tiles are in square c?
- Now add the number of tiles in square a and the number of tiles in square b. Does this equal the number of tiles in square c? If the answer is "yes", then Pythagoras was right!

7. Think

Students should apply the Pythagoras Theorem knowing that:

area of square a (9) + area of square b (16) = area of square c (25)

We can shorten this by saying: $a^2 + b^2 = c^2$

Now apply Pythagoras' Theorem to the right – angled triangle:

$a^2 + b^2 = c^2$

$3^2 + 4^2 = 5^2$

$9 + 16 = 25$

At this stage, students can be given further examples to work on, repeating the above steps with differently sized triangles.

RIB–TT
Ralph's Inquiry – Based Thinking Tool

Description

RIB–TT is a thinking strategy used by Ralph Pirozzo (2011) to scaffold students' learning by using a step – by – step learning sequence ("chunking") from Pre – Knowing to Evaluating. This tool relies heavily on Bloom's Taxonomy (Bloom (ed.), 1956).

Scenario

A primary school teacher wants to use scaffolding to help students create their best stories drawing on *Where the Forest Meets the Sea* (Baker, 1987) for inspiration. RIB – TT has been chosen as the preferred thinking tool because the teacher can "chunk" the learning sequence commencing at the bottom of the chart with Pre – Knowing and finishing with Evaluating.

1. Pre – Knowing level

The teacher shows the students various pages of the book and asks some or all of the following questions.

- What is the title of this book?
- What does the title mean?
- Who is the author of this book?
- Why did the author write this book?
- What is this book about?
- Where does the story take place?
- What can you see on the cover?
- How many different colours can you see?
- Would you like to visit this place?
- Do you recognise the plants?
- What animals can you see?
- Do you know the name of the birds?
- What would these birds eat?
- If you were a parrot, where would you fly to?
- Do you enjoy going to the beach?
- Which animals live in the sea?
- Do you go fishing with your family and/or friends?
- What kind of ecosystem is this?
- Is this book fact or fiction?

2. Knowing level

The teacher reads the book to the students and tries to elicit that stories help us to:

- entertain
- inform
- communicate
- create
- imagine
- dream

RIB–TT (Ralph's Inquiry-Based Thinking Tool)

3. Understanding level

The teacher asks the students why stories are important,, e.g. for communicating, entertaining and informing and provides the students with clear steps on how they can create their own stories. In order to assist the students, the teacher uses Pirozzo's "Narrative Scaffold" (2010).

Narrative Scaffold
Children with Learning Difficulties, ESL Students & Disadvantaged Learners

8. Opinion
How do you feel about the story?

7. Resolution

6. Turning Point

5. Complication
- What is the problem/complication?
- How are we going to solve this problem?

4. Deconstructing Text
- What is the story about?
- Who is the audience?
- Draw characters and setting

3. Orientation

Who	What	Where	When	Why	Vocabulary	Grammar
Characters	Events	Setting (place)	Setting (time)	Reasons		

2. Read Story

4. Deconstructing Text
(Don't underestimate its importance & don't make assumptions about Pre-knowledge)

- Show children how to hold the book and the direction of print
- What do images tell us?
- Listen to stories and retell one's own experiences, thus developing oral language.
- Read and discuss stories together, break them apart using models and create together
- Prompt and use checklists to develop setting and characters
- Pictures and sentence sequencing and labelling
- Provide key words for sentence construction and provide visual and concrete materials (e.g. puppets, story boxes, displays, flashcards and language master)
- Lots of talking/oral language
- Questions and explain metalanguage
- Modelling and deconstructing the text

4. Applying level

The students apply their knowledge and commence working on the first draft of their story by using GLOW and the relevant rubric.

5. Analysing level

The teacher conferences with the students and provides feedback based on the relevant rubric using LDC and/or LITE as the preferred thinking tool.

6. Creating level

The students go back to the first draft of their story and use the teacher's feedback to improve their story. Students should also be encouraged to add something "new and unique" from their own experiences to this second draft.

7. Evaluating level

The teacher conferences with the students in order to assist them to further improve their stories. Students then create a final draft that can be collected for marking and assessment.

SCRAM (Substitute, Combine, Rate, Analyse, Modify)

SCRAM

Substitute, Combine, Rate, Act, Modify

SCRAM

S	C	R	A	M
Separate	Classify	Rate	Act	Magnify
Solve	Combine	Report	Advise	Make
Substitute	Compare	Research	Analyse	Mime
Suggest	Complete	Restate	Apply	Minimise
Survey	Compose	Review	Argue	Modify
	Conduct	Rewrite	Arrange	
	Construct		Assess	
	Contrast		Audition	
	Create			

Description

SCRAM is a versatile thinking tool because different verbs can be selected from each of the five columns depending on the activity that the children are involved in. In order to show how versatile SCRAM can be, four examples will be provided in areas as diverse as English, mathematics and science.

Scenario 1

Rewrite a new version of *The Three Little Pigs* (Stimson, 1996).

- **Substitute** a ferocious lion for one of the little pigs.
- **Create** a story, poem or play about a school bully using *The Three Little Pigs* as inspiration.
- **Rewrite** the story so that the little pigs are not able to climb trees.
- **Audition** for the role of the little pig that lives in the house made of bricks. Use the Rake or a W, X or Y chart to help you prepare.
- **Modify** the story so the little pigs and the wolf live in Cairns, Queensland, where there is no need to have chimneys. How would this have changed the story?

Scenario 2

Using SCRAM to engage children with Cinderella

Substitute — Substitute Cinderella's necklace for her glass slipper.

What impact will this have on the story?

Create — Create a story/poem/play dealing with the story of Cinderella taking place today.

Rewrite — Rewrite the story with the ugly sister finding the slipper instead of the prince.

Audition — Audition for the role of Cinderella or the Prince. Use X, Y, W charts or the Rake to prepare for this audition.

Modify — The Prince comes from a very poor family. Now, retell the story!

SCRAM (Substitute, Combine, Rate, Analyse, Modify)

Scenario 3

Using SCRAM to solve mathematical problems
$C = 2\pi r$

Substitute — Given that in this equation the radius is 5 cm, then substitute for r & find the value of the circumference.

Construct — Construct an experiment that will allow you to estimate the value of π

Reverse — If C = 2 π r then does this mean that 2 π r = C ? Explain.

Apply — A farmer wants to fence two circular fields. One field has a radius of 750 metres & the other has a radius of 1500 metres. As compared to the smaller field, how much more wire will she/he need to fence the larger field?

Modify — Rewrite this formula to find the radius

$$r = \frac{C}{2\pi}$$

Scenario 4

Using SCRAM in Chemical Reactions (Neutralisation)

NaOH + HCl	NaCl + H_2O
S ubstitute	Substitute H_2SO4 for HCl. Predict the products.
C ombine	Balance this chemical reaction & then predict accurately the amount of NaCl produced by combining 250 ml of NaOH & 300 ml of HCl. What will be left in the beaker?
R everse	Reverse this reaction by adding NaCl to H_2O. Will this result in the original chemicals? Thus, is this a reversible chemical reaction?
A dvise	Advise on how you can produce the greatest amount of NaCl & H_2O from this reaction.
M odify	Modify the concentration of HCl. What impact will this have on the rate of this chemical reaction?

SCREAM (Separate, Classify, Rate, Explain, Act, Magnify)

SCREAM
Separate, Classify, Rate, Explain, Act, Magnify

SCREAM

Possible verbs that can be used with this strategy are:

S	C	R	E	A	M
Separate	Classify	Rate	Explain	Act	Magnify
Solve	Combine	Report	Estimate	Advise	Make
Substitute	Compare	Research	Experiment	Analyse	Mime
Suggest	Complete	Restate	Apply	Apply	Minimise
Survey	Compose	Review	Express	Argue	Modify
	Conduct	Rewrite	Empathise	Arrange	
	Construct		Empower	Assess	
	Contrast		Evaluate	Audition	
	Create				

Description

SCRAM was updated to SCREAM in 2008 to incorporate an extra stage to encourage students to explain, estimate etc. The SCRAM scenarios described on the previous pages can be extended using SCREAM as follows.

- Cinderella: The ugly sister finds the slipper instead of the prince. Empathise with the prince. How would he feel? What impact would this have on his search to find a wife?

- Mathematical problems: If r = 5 cm, devise an experiment to prove that C = 2πr. Then, explain how you carried out this experiment and the results that you obtained.

- Chemical reactions: Explain all the variables that impact on the rate of a chemical reaction and provide an example of each.

SOWC analysis
Strengths, Opportunities, Weaknesses, Consequences

SOWC analysis – **S**trengths, **O**pportunities, **W**eaknesses & **C**onsequences

STRENGTHS	OPPORTUNITIES	WEAKNESSES	CONSEQUENCES

Description

SOWC Analysis is the author's interpretation of the well – known SWOT Analysis (Strengths, Weaknesses, Opportunities and Threats). The SWOT Analysis is credited to Albert Humphrey, who used this technique in the 1960s and 1970s using data from Fortune 500 (Humphrey, 2005). The aim of SWOT is to identify the key internal factors (strengths and weaknesses) and external factors (opportunities and threats) that are important in achieving a company's objective.

The author has found that primary and junior secondary students have difficulties in understanding what constitutes a threat; however, they do not have any problems in understanding what a consequence is. Furthermore, primary and junior secondary students find it very useful to align strengths, opportunities, weaknesses and consequences.

SOWC analysis (Strengths, Opportunities, Weaknesses, Consequences)

SOWC analysis is an extremely useful thinking tool that helps students to deal with difficult and controversial issues such as genetic engineering, adoption laws and whether or not Australia should keep refugees in detention centres. The power of SOWC analysis is that students not only brainstorm different ways of dealing with difficult and controversial issues, they actually become involved in solving them by using SOWC analysis level 3.

SOWC analysis level 1 requires students to brainstorm the strengths, opportunities, weaknesses and consequences of an idea or issue. This stage does not solve the issue being discussed. In order to solve the issue, the students need to analyse and prioritise their data through SOWC analysis level 2 and then become personally involved through SOWC analysis level 3.

Scenario

Should we drill for oil and gas in the Great Barrier Reef? Use SOWC to analyse this controversial issue and to make recommendations.

1. SOWC analysis level 1

Students brainstorm the strengths, opportunities, weaknesses and consequences of this issue.

2. SOWC analysis level 2

Having completed SOWC analysis level 1, students are now able to analyse the data, prioritise the most important issues and transfer this data to SOWC analysis level 2.

A maximum of five or six critical issues should appear in each quadrant of SOWC analysis level 2. While working at this level, the students attempt to:

- match strengths to opportunities
- convert weaknesses to strengths
- convert consequences to opportunities

The students should now be able to clearly state what they are going to do to solve this problem.

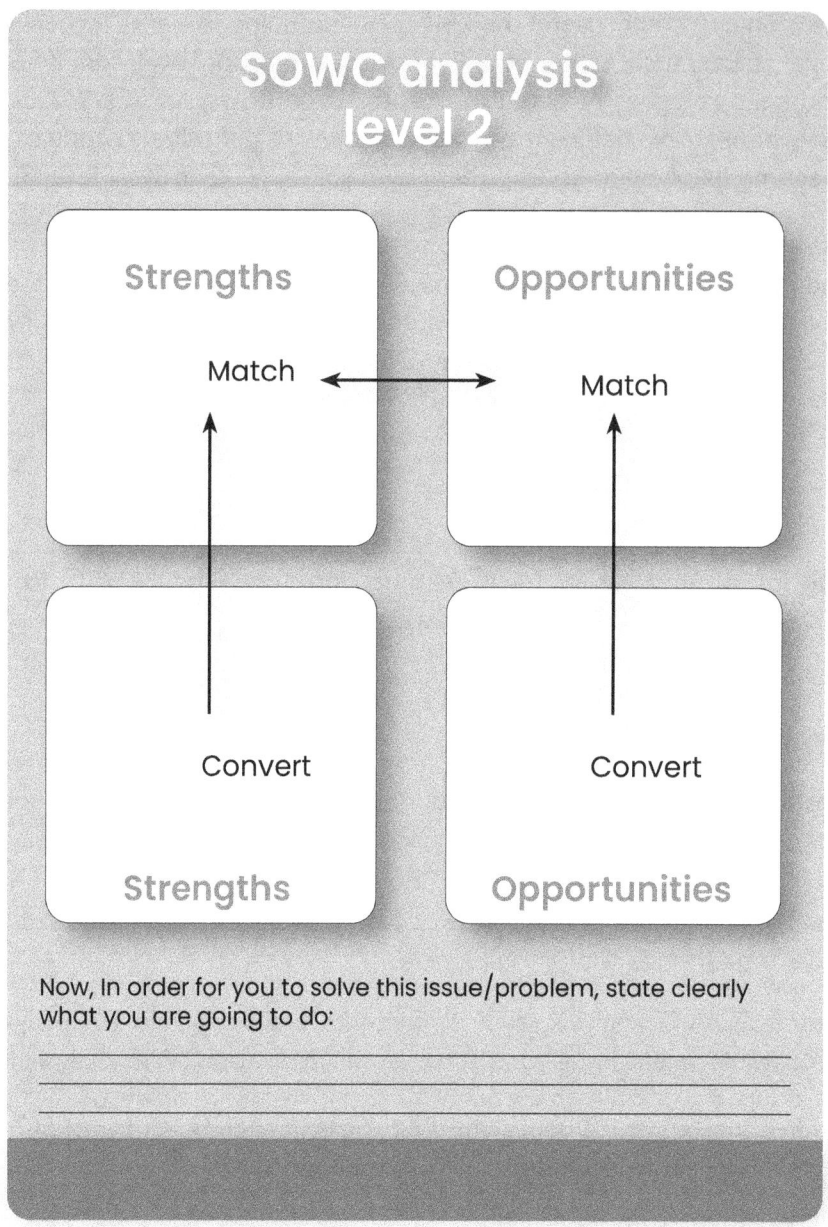

3. SOWC analysis level 3

The students are now ready to move onto SOWC analysis level 3. At this stage, students become personally involved in order to solve the issue. Students discuss the following questions:

- What activities will be undertaken?
- How will these activities be completed?
- Who will complete each activity?
- When will these activities be completed?
- Will there be any costs involved?

SOWC analysis (Strengths, Opportunities, Weaknesses, Consequences)

SOWC analysis – level 3
What will you do to solve this problem?

WHAT?	HOW?	WHO?	WHEN?	COSTS?

Extension activities

- Why should we have rules in our classroom?
- How can we deal effectively with bullying?
- Should Australia be involved in the war in Afghanistan?
- Should euthanasia be legalised?
- Should space exploration continue?
- Should human cloning be allowed?
- Should we have school uniforms?
- Do you think we should set up separate classes for boys and girls?
- Should refugees be kept in detention centres?
- Experts are predicting that the cost of one barrel of oil will reach $200. What impact will this have on our economy?
- What can countries do to stop global warming? What can each individual do to prevent global warming?
- Should we help Africa to eliminate poverty?
- Should every Australian receive $10,000 a year regardless of whether they work or not?

STIESA

Show, Think, Imitate, Explore, Sound, Apply

S Show	T Think	I Imitate	E Explore	S Sound	A Apply
The teacher will show the children (modelling), e.g. story pictures & generating and rehearsing a play	The student needs to think in meaning or images in both languages, e.g. flashcards	The students will imitate/copy the teacher by doing what the teacher is doing, e.g. reading the story line from Red Riding Hood	The student will explore by looking, touching and feeling, e.g. drawing from experience (emotional memory), reading texts, feelings, touching (pretend) things in the story	The student will sound it out (pronunciation, articulation, practising & perfecting the sounds)	The student will apply their knowledge by recasting in a new speaking situation

A possible learning sequence for Spoken Language Acquisition

Description

STIESA provides teachers with a possible learning sequence that can be used to assist children during spoken language acquisition. It involves six stages. Three different scenarios dealing with *The Three Little Pigs*, Aboriginal Dreamtime stories and assessing the emotional levels of EAL/D children will be provided, to show how valuable STIESA is in assisting children during spoken language acquisition.

Scenario 1

The teacher is using *The Three Little Pigs* (Stimson, 1996) to aid students in improving their language proficiency. The teacher has chosen to use STIESA because it provides six different ways of engaging students in their learning.

STIESA (Show, Think, Imitate, Explore, Sound, Apply)

1. Show

The teacher shows the book to the students and asks the following questions:

- What do you see?
- What is the title of the story?
- What do you think the story is about?
- Who are the main characters?

2. Think

The teacher reads the book to the students and uses flash cards to stimulate the students' thinking about the three little pigs, the wolf and the materials used to make the three different houses. The teacher creates a word bank: huffed, puffed, by the hair of my chinny chin chin, frightened, furious, clambered, roundabout, butter churn and splash.

3. Imitate

Students imitate by re – reading the text with the teacher and singing at the appropriate places. Students can also match sequence cards and read the flash cards aloud in order to improve their pronunciation and facial expressions.

4. Explore

Students explore by constructing three little houses: one using straw, one using sticks and one using bricks (use wooden blocks instead of bricks).

5. Sound

The teacher encourages the students to a shared book experience and encourages them to sound repeated text, e.g. "I'll huff and I'll puff!").

6. Apply

The students apply their knowledge by:

- drawing and building a cyclone – proof house
- retelling the story using puppets
- acting the story by choosing to be one of the three little pigs or the wolf
- retelling the story with the wolf eating the little pig that lives in the house made of bricks

Scenario 2

The teacher is using STIESA to encourage the students to write their own text based on a number of Aboriginal Dreamtime stories.

1. Show

The teacher shows various Dreamtime stories to the students and then reads *How the Birds Got Their Colours* (Albert, 2004) to the students. The students are then asked to look at the characteristics of the Aboriginal artwork and listen to the music that accompanies the story.

2. Think

The students use pictures to tell a new story.

3. Imitate

Students provide examples from their own experiences and are involved in shared reading to improve their pronunciation and facial expressions.

4. Explore

Use the Rake to deconstruct one of the scenes in the book and to actually "place" the students "there".

5. Sound

The students use the text to role – play a scene from the book.

6. Apply

The students apply their knowledge by:

- writing their own play based on a jointly constructed Dreamtime story
- performing their play
- making a sound map of a Dreamtime story
- creating their own artwork depicting their favourite scene from the story

STIESA (Show, Think, Imitate, Explore, Sound, Apply)

Scenario 3

The teacher is using STIESA to assess the emotional levels of EAL/D students.

1. Show

The teacher shows the students flash cards of eyes and faces showing various expressions such as:

- happy
- sad
- afraid
- calm
- angry
- joyful
- cold
- hot
- proud
- embarrassed
- hungry
- full

2. Think

The students are encouraged to think in both English and their native language. The teacher asks them to focus on the "feelings" represented on each flash card.

3. Imitate

While holding various flash cards, the students are asked to imitate the teacher's facial expressions and body language for each of the feelings listed above.

4. Explore

The students explore their feelings by drawing about a time when they were happy, sad, afraid etc.

5. Sound

The students practise the sounds by saying and repeating words about feelings: happy, sad, afraid etc.

6. Apply

The students then apply what they have learnt by drawing and writing about what makes them feel happy, sad, afraid etc.

TAP
Think All Possibilities

Think all possibilities

This thinking tool can be used to encourage children to brainstorm how different individuals feel about the same issue.

TAP (Think All Possibilities)

Description

This thinking tool has been designed to encourage children to brainstorm as many ideas as possible. It can also be used to encourage students to brainstorm different points of view and how different individuals feel about the same issue.

The TAP is an inquiry – based thinking tool. For example, it encourages children to brainstorm different ways to design a cover page for their reports or to empathise with a particular person or character.

Scenario

It has been suggested that the school day should be longer, starting at 8.00 a.m. and finishing at 5.00 p.m. This would ensure children were safe and appropriately supervised for longer, helping the increasing number of homes where two parents are working. The extra time in the school day could be used to encourage fitness and outdoor activities, and ensure that homework is completed.

1. Organise the children into groups and let them choose one of the following roles, which will help each group to think of all the different viewpoints:

   - student
   - parent or guardian
   - teacher
   - principal
   - public transport official

2. Allow the students five to ten minutes to prepare themselves for their roles.

3. Encourage the students to share their ideas and responses to the issue in their groups.

4. Carry out a class debate or discussion.

5. Review with the class how this strategy helped them to deepen their thinking.

TEAM
Think, Explain, Arrange, Make

TEAM

T hink about the issue, problem or challenge

E xplain and evaluate

A rrange

M ake, modify, maximise, minimise

Description

TEAM was devised specifically to involve students in making a product by encouraging them to go through a four – stage thinking process that involves:

1. thinking about the issue, problem or challenge

2. explaining and/or evaluating the issue

3. arranging the materials

4. making, modifying, maximising or minimising the product

TEAM (Think, Explain, Arrange, Make)

Scenario

The teacher provides groups of students with the following materials to design, build and test their own hot air balloon.

- one large plastic bag (72 litres)
- two small paper cups
- a pair of scissors
- masking tape
- four pieces of smooth string (each piece should be 50 cm long)
- a hair dryer (ensure that the hair dryer is used by an adult)

1. Think

Using the thinking clouds (p. 80) or TAP (p. 72), brainstorm different ways that you could build a hot air balloon using all the materials provided.

2. Explain

As a group, choose the best method from the brainstorming activity and explain to your teacher and/or another group why you have selected this method and how you are going to build your hot air balloon.

3. Arrange

- Decide how you are going to arrange all the materials provided to build your hot air balloon.
- Draw a diagram of your hot air balloon, showing how it will be constructed, and show it to your teacher and/or another group to receive feedback using LDC and/or LITE.
- Based on the feedback received, make the necessary improvements to your drawing.

4. Make

Make your hot air balloon by working cooperatively with your group.

- How will you work together to build the hot air balloon?
- How have the different jobs been allocated?
- How was this decision made?

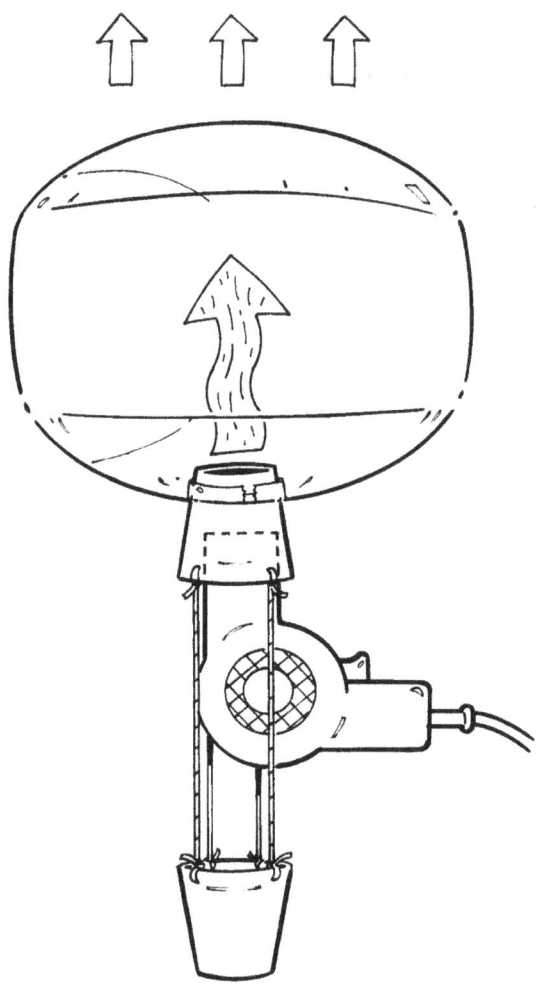

Reflection

Did your hot air balloon work? If so, explain why the hot air balloon rises in the air. If not, suggest ways that the design could be improved.

Predict what would happen to your balloon if you were to use:

- a smaller or larger bag
- a bag that is made of heavier or lighter material
- cups made of styrofoam instead of paper
- a more or less powerful hair dryer
- a hair dryer that produces only cold air

You live in a two – storey house. On an extremely hot day, where would you find the coolest part of the house to sleep in? Why?

The Rake

Description

The Rake has six aspects, one each for touch, smell, taste, sight, hearing and feelings (emotions). The Rake is a useful tool for guiding the children's thought processes and helping them to improve their writing by adding detail and structure.

Scenario

A Year 9 history teacher is teaching a unit on the Anzacs to a group of 30 boys who are very reluctant to read and write. The teacher has decided to use the Rake in order to immerse the students in this topic, and then proceeds to do the following.

1. Show the students a variety of films, videos, photographs and posters related to World War I (1914–1918);

2. Read the students excerpts from various letters and books including *The Silver Donkey* (Hartnett, 2004) and ask a number of questions:

- Who was John Simpson Kirkpatrick?
- What was so special about Simpson and his donkey?
- Why is Simpson described as Australia's most publicly known Anzac?
- What characteristics did Simpson display that have made him such an integral part of the Anzac spirit?

3. Provide students with pictures showing them what it was like for soldiers to live in the trenches during WWI, and encourage them to visit www.firstworldwar.com. Then, a class discussion should follow relating to the soldiers' experiences of living in the trenches. Ask them questions, including:

- What would the soldiers' feet be like after weeks and weeks in the trenches?
- How did the soldiers stay in touch with their loved ones in Australia?
- How were they treated by the officers?
- Where did the soldiers sleep?
- What were they given to eat?
- What about the smell?
- Where did they wash?
- Where did they go to the toilet?
- How did they get rid of lice?

4. Instruct the students to search for "trench warfare" in Google Images. Allow them a few minutes to view these outstanding photographs, then encourage students to imagine what life would be like in the trenches. Then use butcher's paper or the whiteboard to register students' comments on the Rake, from the previous page. Using the information collected in the brainstorming session, the students are then instructed to create one of the following:

- a letter to a loved one describing life in the trenches
- a letter to the editor of your local newspaper
- a diary
- an interview
- a *PowerPoint* presentation
- a poster or diorama
- a jingle or rap

Extension activities

1. You are visiting Antarctica and you find that you have lost your group. Use the Rake to describe your experience and then write a letter to your parents or your best friend sharing with them how you have survived in Antarctica.

2. The area of the village, town or city in which you live has been flooded and your family has been evacuated to the local secondary school hall. Your mum and two younger sisters are with you, but your father is missing. The Salvation Army has set up their mobile kitchen in the hall and you are now sharing the toilet facilities with 500 other people. Unfortunately, due to the large number of people using the toilets, they are no longer flushing and their contents are spilling onto the concrete floors. Use the Rake to deconstruct this scene and then write a letter to the editor of your local newspaper describing in detail what is taking place.

The Rake

TOUCH	SMELL	TASTE	LOOK	LISTEN	FEEL	THINK
What do the objects **feel** like?	What do you **smell** like?	What does it **taste** like?	What do you **see**?	What sounds do you **hear**?	How do you **feel**?	What are you **thinking**?
- mud - dead - bodies - vomit - guts - blood - rags - rats - trenches - sandbags - biscuits - water - bottles - guns - bayonet - letter from home	- rotting flesh - petrol - vulgar smells - body odours - latrine bucket - vomit - gun powder - urine & faeces - gangrene - rotting - garbage - farts - stale food - putrid water - death	- spam - tasteless - leathery - bland - gritty - slippery - dry - soggy - salty - sour - mouldy - maggots & weevils - stale water	- flag - periscope - comrades - helmets - smoke - shots - ocean - walls & cliffs - wounded - soldiers - desolate - land - barbed wires - trenches - dead bodies - graves - mud - blood & guts	- blasting - screaming - shouting - agony - gunfire - feet sloshing in trenches - swearing - yelling - bullets - cannons - officers barking orders - frustration	- let down - distressed - feeling cheated - despair - hungry - lost - scared - anxious - sad - stunned - proud - bold - desperation - longing for home	- Yes Sir, I will - how will I survive? - I am going to die - what the future holds - I should have stayed at home - I can do this - I'm coming to help you - I really want to see her again - I want to go home

Thinking clouds

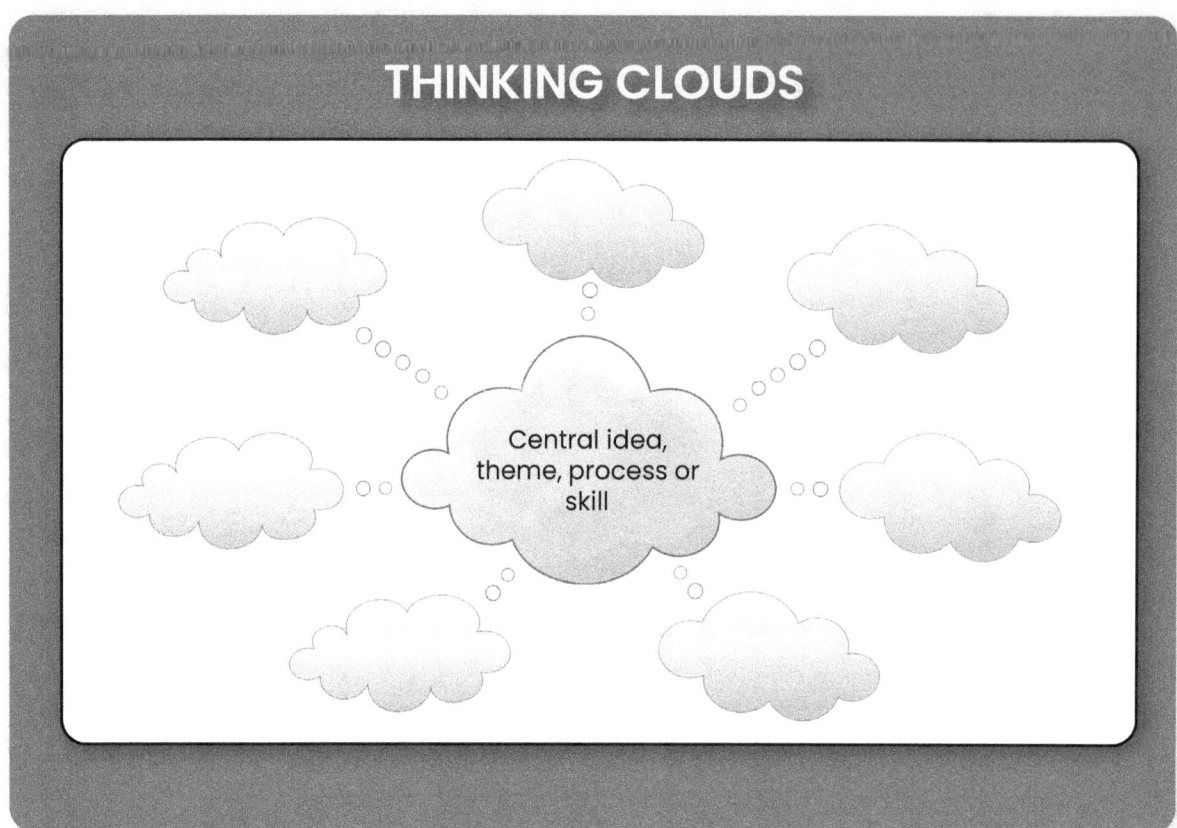

Description

Thinking clouds are used to represent students' thinking as a map. This is a brain – friendly way for the students to follow their thoughts. Thinking clouds promote divergent thinking. They encourage students to dream, brainstorm and be highly imaginative and creative.

Thinking clouds are similar to the mindmaps developed through the work of Nancy Margulies as fun, interactive ways to get ideas on paper (Margulies, 1992). However, the author has found that the term 'thinking clouds' is very useful when working with young students.

Thinking clouds can be used to break down a written text or to brainstorm ideas around a central theme or topic.

Scenario 1

Brainstorm all the places in the world where you could get "lost" and then write and/or draw this information using thinking clouds. You will need at least ten entries.

Thinking clouds

Scenario 2

Brainstorm all the animals and plants that can live in a freshwater food web.

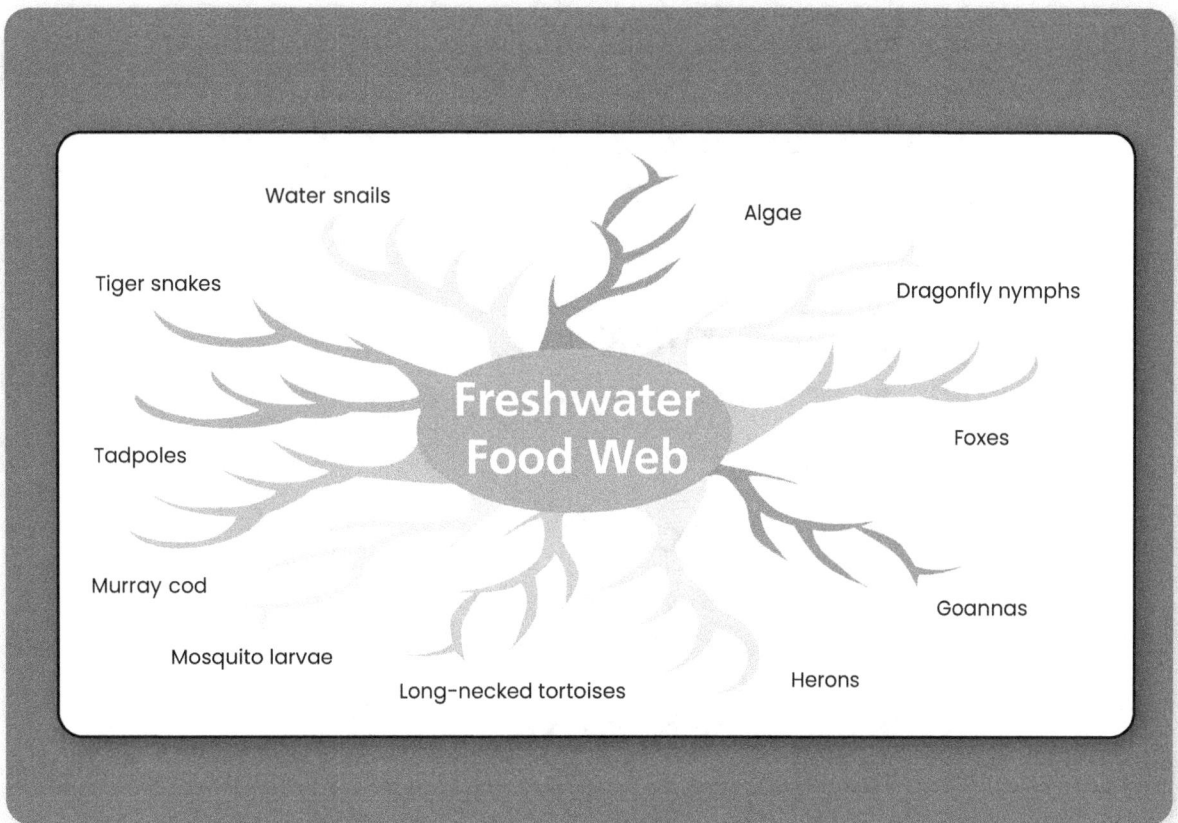

Reflection

The thinking clouds tool is a brainstorming technique that helps the brain to generate huge numbers of ideas and possibilities. However, while it is extremely useful in assisting students to generate ideas, many students do very little with these ideas. The reason for this is that the students are unable to harness the energy that was created by using the thinking clouds. Whenever possible, teachers should use thinking clouds to generate ideas ("energy") and then use concept maps to harness this energy. This method will help students develop effective and efficient problem-solving techniques.

TREC

Think, Read, Estimate, Calculate

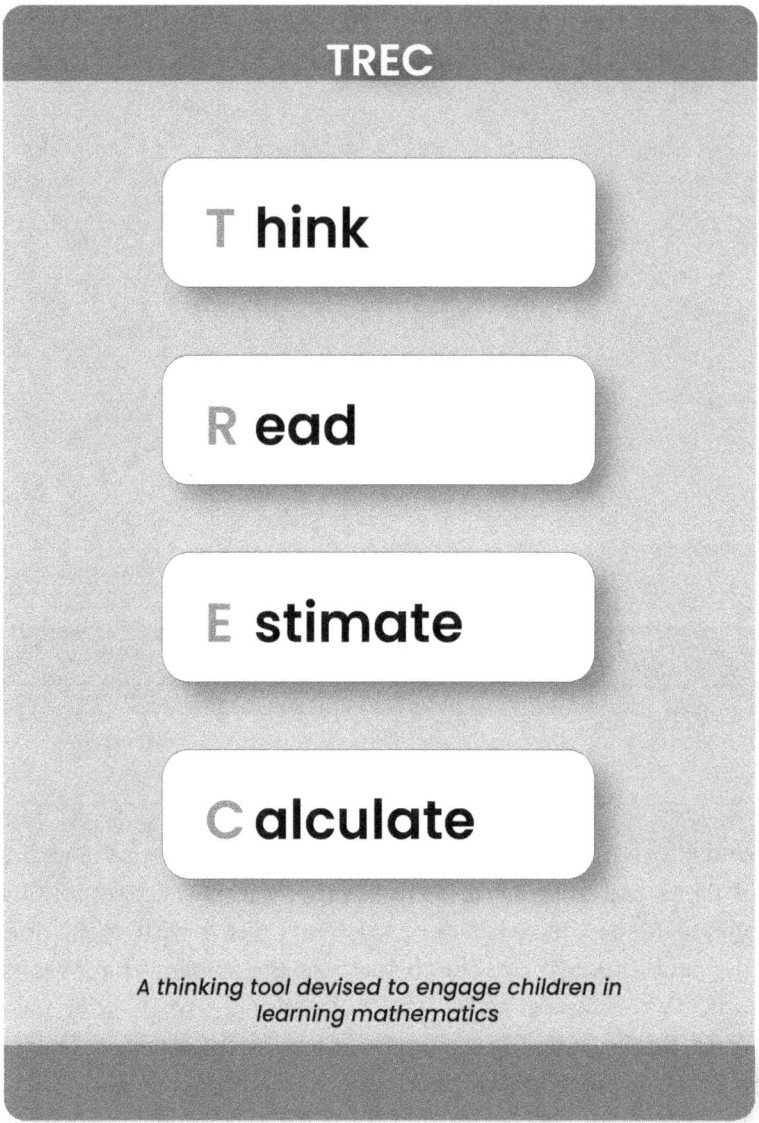

Description

TREC involves students in a four – stage framework that directs them to:

1. Think carefully about the problem to be solved.

2. Read the question carefully and discuss the problem with other students until they understand what is involved in the task.

3. Estimate the answer.

4. Carry out the required calculation.

TREC (Think, Read, Estimate, Calculate)

TREC is particularly useful to scaffold students into doing mathematics. This tool ensures that students know what they need to do by encouraging them to go through a four – stage approach. One of the critical stages is for the students to fully understand the problem that they have to solve. Thus, TREC encourages the students to read the question carefully. If they still don't understand it, they read it again and discuss it with their group. Finally, they may ask their teacher for assistance.

Scenario 1

You are the accountant in a small boat – building business. The designers have come up with a new boat design and you have been asked to provide a cost for building the boat. Use Trec to help you do the costing:

1. Think about the numbers involved in doing the costing.

2. Read the question carefully. How is the boat going to be built? What will need to be included in the costs, e.g. materials and labour?

3. Estimate what the cost of building the boat is likely to be.

4. Calculate the total cost of building the boat.

Scenario 2

A Year 7 maths teacher has asked the students to find the perimeter of their classroom and has decided that TREC will be useful in achieving the aim of this activity.

1. Think

- What does "perimeter" mean? If you do not know, find out by searching the internet or reading the relevant pages of books selected by your teacher.
- Use thinking clouds to carry out a class brainstorming activity.
- What is "perimeter" used for in the real world?
- Use Think, pair, share and/or Think, pair, share, square (p. 106-109) with your group or class to discover who in the community uses the term "perimeter".
- How can you find the perimeter of your:
    (a) classroom?
    (b) desk?
    (c) windows?
    (d) whiteboard?
    (e) playground area?
    (f) hall?
    (g) football field?

2. Read

- Read the question provided by your teacher.
- What is the question asking you to do?
- In order to find the perimeter of an object, what information do you need?

3. Estimate

- How can you estimate the perimeter of your:
    - (a) classroom?
    - (b) desk?
    - (c) windows?
    - (d) whiteboard?
    - (e) playground area?
    - (f) hall?
    - (g) football field?
- What instruments can you use to estimate your answers?
- How have you come up with your answers?
- Compare your answers to that of your group/class. Is there a wide range of answers? Why or why not?

4. Calculate

- Calculate the perimeter of your classroom.
- Are there different ways of calculating the perimeter? List the different methods that can be used and then demonstrate them to your group/class.
- Record your working in your notebook. Compare with your group/class.
- How do you know that you have found the right answer?
- Compare your answer with that of your group or class. Is it the same?
- Is your answer similar/dissimilar to your estimate? Why or why not?

Reflection

- Could you use the knowledge you have gained from this activity in everyday situations?
- Is the ability to calculate the perimeter of an object important? Brainstorm all the different people in your community who may need to know how to calculate perimeter.

Venn diagram

Venn diagram: compare and contrast

These characteristics belong to A only | These characteristics are shared by both A & B | These characteristics belong to B only

Description

Venn diagrams were introduced by John Venn (1834–1923) in a paper entitled 'On the Diagrammatic and Mechanical Representation of Propositions and Reasonings', published in 1880 in the *Philosophical Magazine and Journal of Science*. Venn used these diagrams to teach elementary set theory, as well as to illustrate simple set relationships in probability, statistics, linguistics and computer science. The first person to use the term 'Venn diagram' was Clarence Irving Lewis in *A Survey of Symbolic Logic* (1918).

Venn diagrams have been used by teachers for many years in helping students to compare and contrast.

Scenario 1

Your grandparents are moving to a retirement village where space is extremely limited. However, they love animals and are determined to take one pet with them. Their preferred animals are cats and dogs. Based on the results of the Venn diagram, which animal should your grandparents take to the retirement village? Why?

DOGS
Smooth tongue
Bark
Canine
Short whiskers
Omnivore
Swim in water
No claws
Train easily
Some dribble
Need more attention
Don't climb
Well domesticated

Pets
Mammals
Live babies
Hair and fur
Whiskers
Eat meat
Domesticated

CATS
Rough tongue
Meow, purr
Feline
Long whiskers
Carnivore
Partially domesticated
Climb
Bury faeces
Retractable claws
Sharp claws
Groom themselves
Need less attention
Don't train easily

Scenario 2

Teachers can also use the Venn diagram as a pre – and post – test to find out:

- what students already know about a certain topic at the beginning of the unit; and
- what students have learnt by the end of the unit

For example, before a unit on plants and animals is taught, the teacher can ascertain what the students already know by asking them to complete a Venn diagram. The teacher then collects the children's work, dates it and stores it for later comparison. At the end of this unit, the teacher asks the students to complete another Venn diagram on plants and animals. By comparing the first Venn diagram with the second, teachers will get a very good idea of how effective their teaching has been.

Scenario 3

The students can choose any of the following and then list the differences and similarities using a Venn diagram.

Compare and Contrast	
telephone	mobile phone
day	night
winter	summer
evil	good
democracy	dictatorship
leader	follower
friend	enemy
old	new
dishonest	honest

WASPS
Watch, Ask, Show, Practise, Show

WASPS

W atch me *(Teacher)*

A sk me *(Teacher ⇄ student)*

S how. Now I will show you how! *(Teacher)*

P ractise, practise and practise some more *(Student)*

S how. Now you show me how! *(Student ⇄ teacher)*

WASPS (Watch, Ask, Show, Practise, Show)

Description

WASPS can be used in all practical domains such as PE, industrial arts, science, agricultural studies, art and food technology/home economics by taking the children through five steps:

1. watch me (students watch the teacher)
2. ask me (students ask the teacher questions)
3. show (teacher shows the students)
4. practise (students try for themselves)
5. show (students show the teacher)

A physical education Head Teacher, is teaching a unit dealing with effective communication and skills needed for this. She is using WASPS as follows:

Scenario 1: WASPS in PDHPE: Coded communication

Many types of communication have existed throughout history. This section will focus on coded communication.

Activate the students' natural curiosity about secrets and secret codes by asking them if they have ever encountered, used or created a secret code. Tell the students that they have already encountered cryptology if they use SMS. For example, "u" is often used for "you" and "btw" is used for "by the way". Encourage students to give more examples of instances where they might encounter cryptology. Make a collaborative list of the "codes" they use on their phones, in email or on social networking sites, and superficially explore reasons why they abbreviate, or code, their communication.

Discuss with the students how codes are a type of communication that is secret. While it can be used just for fun, secret codes have also been used during wartime.

Notes for workbooks:

Codes are languages used by people to secretly communicate with one another. Codes are designed to hide a message by using numbers, letters, words, symbols, sounds or signals to represent actual text.

1. Watch me (teacher)

A Pigpen code is a type of cipher that was used during the American Civil War. Since the "code" resembled pig pens, if the message was intercepted by the enemy it would merely look like a farmer's diagram. A Pigpen code uses symbols and dots to replace letters of the alphabet. Although it can be easily deciphered, changing the arrangement of the alphabet increases how complex your codes can become.

Write up a Pigpen code on the board, following the instructions below. Explain to the students what it is and how it was used. Show a specific example.

Step 1: Start by creating the "Pigpen" key by drawing two noughts and crosses grids and two large Xs side by side (see the diagram below). Now write the letters of the alphabet A–Z starting with the grids and ending with the two X shapes (see the diagram below). In the second version of both the grid and the X shape, place a distinctive dot in each box as shown on the diagram. It is very important that each dot is in exactly the same place as the dots in the diagram below. You now have the base of the Pigpen code.

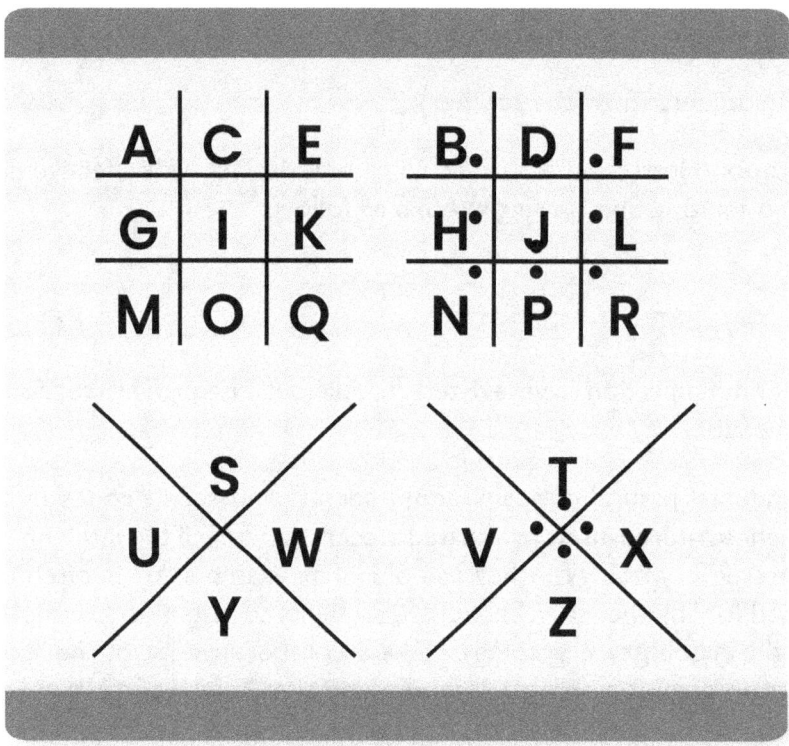

Step 2: When writing a letter of the alphabet using the code, the relevant "pen" is used without the letter in it. For example:

☐• = a square box with four sides and a dot centred at the bottom would be a "J"

☐ = a square box with four sides and no dot would be an "I"

So, the word "HELLO" in Pigpen code would look like this:

2. Ask me (teacher–students)

Invite the students to ask questions to clarify how the code works.

3. Show (teacher)

Using the example given, demonstrate to the students how the Pigpen code works. Write the first two letters of a word in code and ask the students to finish the rest. Give them a time limit. Discuss the solution with all the students.

4. Practise (students)

Allow the students to get creative and practise using the code. Each student creates a coded message, then swaps with a partner and tries to decipher their partner's message. Encourage the students to use sentences rather than just words. Besides increasing difficulty, this also increases literacy as students need to decipher words, spaces and sentence structure. To further increase difficulty, have the students change the order of the grids in their original code. The letters must still appear in order A–Z. See the diagram below as an example:

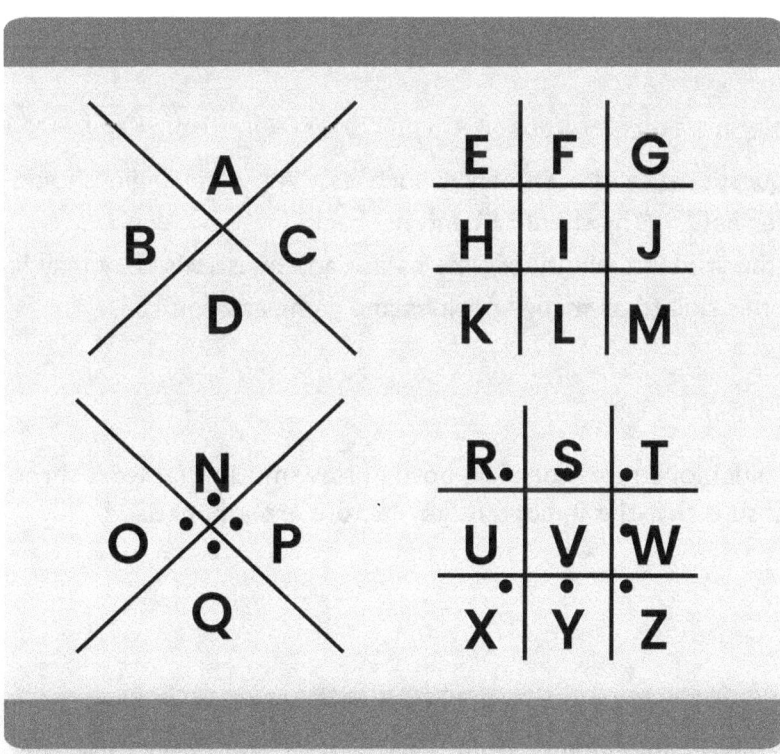

5. Show (students)

Students demonstrate their codes to the class, explore their level of difficulty and discuss the positives and negatives of coded communication. When discussing these issues, focus on the communication process, such as the importance of two – way communication and message clarity. Debate the points for and against the effectiveness of the Pigpen code.

Scenario 2: WASPS in PDHPE: Track, Catch and Throw

Practical lessons in PDHPE lend themselves to the use of WASPS as a structured tool to ensure students comprehend the skill and can demonstrate their understanding. In this scenario, WASPS is used to teach and improve the students' hand – eye coordination through "Track, Catch and Throw".

1. Watch me (teacher)

In this process, the teacher begins the lesson by explaining the technique to use for an effective catch of the ball and throw back to the receiver:

- track with your eyes until the ball is safely in your hands
- release by drawing back your throwing arm to a right angle
- throw your arm forward, following through to your opposite knee, bending the back.

2. Ask me (teacher–students)

- Pose questions to the students, such as: "At what angle should my arm and shoulder be?" "Why should I bend my back?"
- Allow the students plenty of time to ask any questions they may have.
- Relate this skill to as many activities and games as you can.

3. Show (teacher)

The teacher then demonstrates the skill, both in slow motion (at least three times) and at normal speed. Ensure that the important key factors are emphasised.

4. Practise (students)

Devise an activity for the students to practise the throwing technique, such as:

- Paired throwing: students stand in a straight line, with their partners standing opposite them, about five metres away. Allow plenty of space between students for wild throws etc. A soft ball should be used, such as a tennis ball or bean bag, if hand–eye coordination is not apparent.

WASPS (Watch, Ask, Show, Practise, Show)

- Hit the target practice: set up a target for each group of students. Have a student (Student A) stand next to the target. Student A throws the ball to the waiting student (Student B) approximately five to ten metres back. Student B tracks the ball, catches it and returns the throw in an attempt to hit the target. Each ring on the target has a value and teams count up their points at the end of the activity. Keep a running score for the groups or the whole class. The students try to improve their score each week.

5. Show (students)

Incorporate the skills into any game that uses the concept of tracking and throwing, such as t – ball, dodge ball, bin ball etc. Modify the game to begin with so that students experience success with their skill. This can be achieved by:

- using larger balls
- increasing or decreasing the playing area
- using smaller group numbers to begin with
- modifying the rules e.g. play T-ball rather than softball

Once the students have developed better hand–eye coordination, make the game harder by decreasing the size of the ball, increasing the field size etc.

The author is grateful to Mrs Nicole Crowe for her permission to include the activities outlined in WASPS in this book.

WINCE

Want, Identify, Need, Create, Evaluate

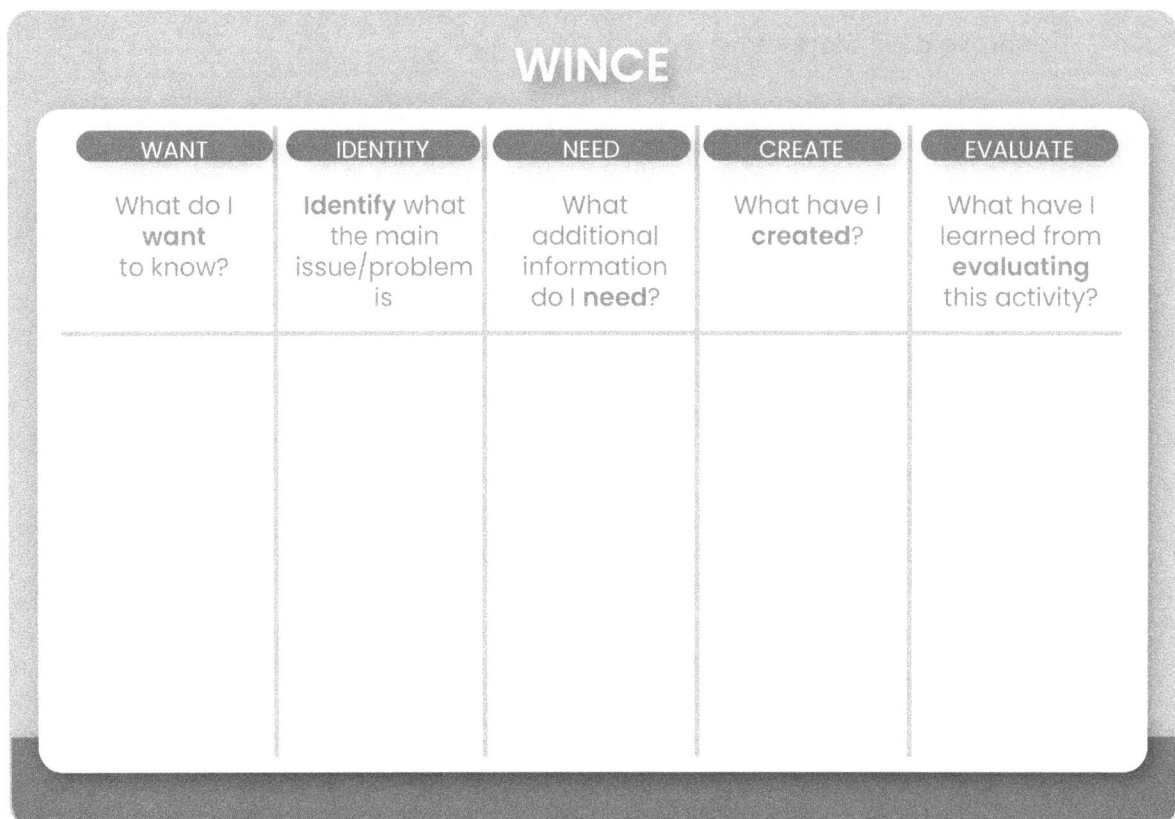

Description

The WINCE strategy is a five – stage problem – solving process.

1. Establish what the students would like to know.

2. Identify the challenge or problem to be solved.

3. Decide on extra information that may be needed.

4. Create a solution.

5. Evaluate what the students have learnt

This strategy can be used in any area for problem solving by identifying the key question and the important skills needed to solve the problem.

WINCE (Want, Identify, Need, Create, Evaluate)

Scenario 1

The aim of this experiment is to challenge the students to see if they can use WINCE to find a way of floating a potato half way up a bucket of water, without using any weights and/or strings and by keeping the level of the water at 2 cm below the top of the bucket. One way of achieving this is to use the information that the students have gathered by carrying out the potato experiment using the PSDR method (pp. 49-50). However, the students will need an additional bucket. This will be referred to as bucket C. This bucket is similar in size to buckets A and B.

- Divide the students into groups of three and allow them to brainstorm this problem for ten minutes using thinking clouds. Each group elects a "reporter" who will brief the rest of the class on how they will solve this problem based on the results obtained from the thinking clouds. The groups work through the steps outlined in WINCE to carry out this challenge.

Recently, the author noticed two groups of Year 7 students solving this problem using very different techniques:

- Group A: This group poured enough salty water from bucket B into bucket C until it was half full. The potato then floated in the middle of the bucket. Then, ice cubes were added until the water level reached 2 cm below the top of the bucket while the potato floated in the middle of the bucket.
- Group B: This group poured enough salty water from bucket B into bucket C until it was half full and the potato floated in the middle of the bucket. Then, they placed it in a freezer overnight. The next day, the water was frozen with the potato in the middle of the bucket. The students then added water until the water level reached 2 cm below the top of the bucket.

Reflection

1. In your opinion, which group(s) achieved the aim of this experiment?
2. What other techniques could you have used to achieve this aim?
3. In addition to the thinking clouds and WINCE, which other thinking tools could have been used to solve this problem?
4. What did you learn by solving this problem?

Scenario 2

A special chair needs to built for a disabled child. Use WINCE to design and build this chair and evaluate whether or not it will be suitable for this child.

W chart

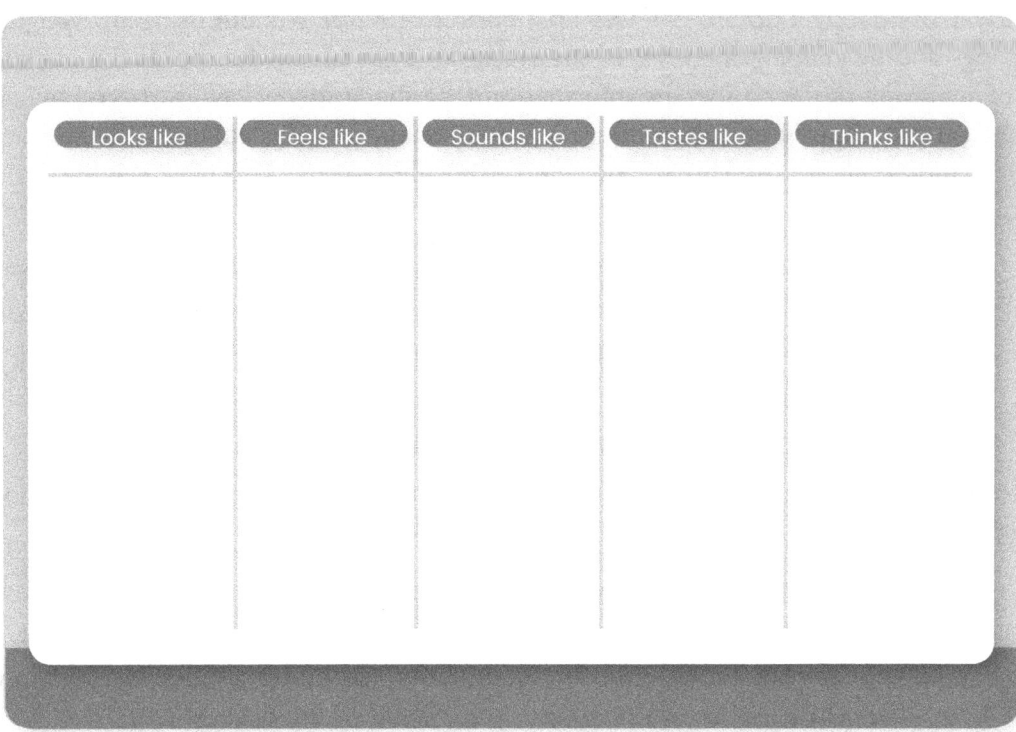

Description

The W chart has five aspects – what you see, feel, hear, taste and think. This is particularly important in describing food. This tool can be used for:

- creating recipes and menus
- cooking
- setting up a coffee shop or restaurant for hospitality and tourism students
- celebrating children's birthdays
- celebrating special events, such as Australia Day

Scenario 1

Present a role – play to describe the best or the worst meal you have ever eaten.

Divide the students into groups of three or four. Have each group complete the following questions on the W chart:

- How did the food look?
- How did you feel when you were eating the meal?
- What sounds did you hear? What were people saying?
- How did the meal taste?
- What thoughts went through your mind?

Have each group practise their role – play before presenting to the class.

An Australia Day W chart

Feels Like
- slapping mosquitoes
- sticky lemonade
- swatting flies
- prickly grass
- humid
- hot

Tastes Like
- bread and butter
- mum's yucky coleslaw
- caramelised onions
- sausages/rissoles
- tomato sauce
- charcoal

Looks Like
- outside
- dad cooking
- smoke/flames
- burnt rissoles

Sounds like
- sizzling food
- mum laughing
- tongs clicking
- kids yelling
- dad yelling
- glasses clinking

Thinks Like
- Another family BBQ
- How much longer will they stay?
- I wonder what my friends are doing?
- Why are BBQ sausages always black?
- How many sausages will an average Australian eat in a lifetime?

Scenario 2

Your parents are having a family barbecue. Complete the W chart to describe your experiences.

Scenario 3

Today, the teacher and your fellow students are celebrating your birthday. Your mum has brought a chocolate cake to the school. Complete the W chart to describe what you experience as you walk into the classroom.

X chart

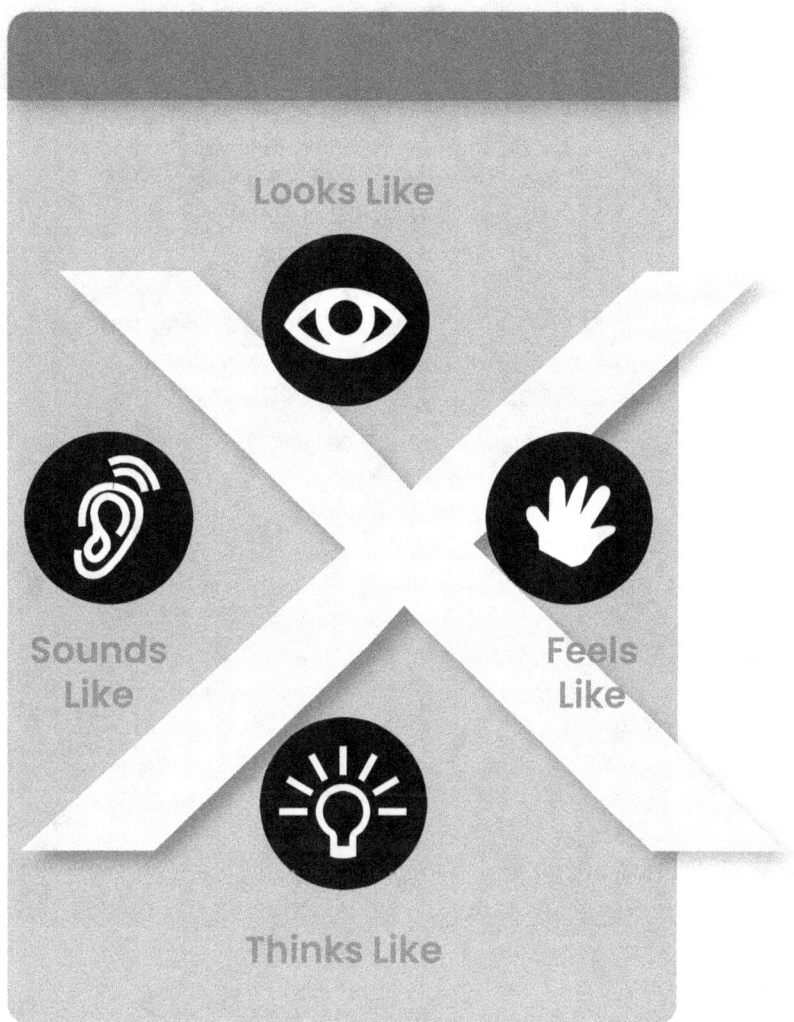

Description

The X chart is similar to the Y chart (pp. 101 – 102) but provides an extra dimension. The X chart adds thoughts as the fourth dimension. Students can record their ideas about what they see, feel, hear and think. This is particularly important for adding an affective aspect to the scenario being described.

Teachers can also use the X chart to deconstruct a character in a book, film or play. This should be followed by creating a story and/or a drama presentation.

Scenario 1

A group of students are bullying you in the playground. Use the X chart to describe what you see, hear and feel, and what you are thinking.

Student bullying X chart

👁 Looks Like
- Angry faces
- Insecure/scared
- Small/vulnerable
- Oppressed/worthless
- Hunched shoulders
- Mean/angry
- Withdrawn
- Following me
- Pulling faces
- Crowd building up
- People rushing in
- Being surrounded
- Everybody is staring at me
- Pointing/pushing
- Long/sad face
- Punching
- Defenceless
- Crying

👂 Sounds Like
- Loud sobbing
- Arguing
- Slamming
- Screaming
- Threatening
- Taunting
- Intimidating
- Harsh voices
- Foul language
- Negative messages
- Leave me alone
- Cheering/Booing
- Name calling
- Whispering
- Ridiculing
- Swearing
- Laughing
- Teasing
- Nah nah

✋ Feels Like
- Fear/Terror
- Doesn't exist
- Scared/Sad
- Misunderstood
- Picked on
- Helpless
- Embarrassed
- Afraid/Hurt
- Depressed/Suicidal
- Insignificant
- Cornered
- Sickening
- Intimidated
- Trapped
- Loser
- Lonely
- Isolated
- Frightened
- Powerless
- Singled out
- Victimised
- Ashamed

💡 Thinks Like
- How can I stop this?
- Unfair – Why me?
- I've had enough – I can't go on
- How can I get away?
- What am I supposed to do?
- No-one knows what it's like
- What's wrong with me?
- Where am I safe?
- I don't want to be here
- I don't want to come to school tomorrow
- Who can help?
- I can't tell anyone
- Everybody hates me
- What have I done?
- I hate myself and them
- I can't win
- I am worthless
- How can I escape?
- I have no friends
- Not my fault
- How do I survive?
- I am a failure
- No-one likes me

Y chart

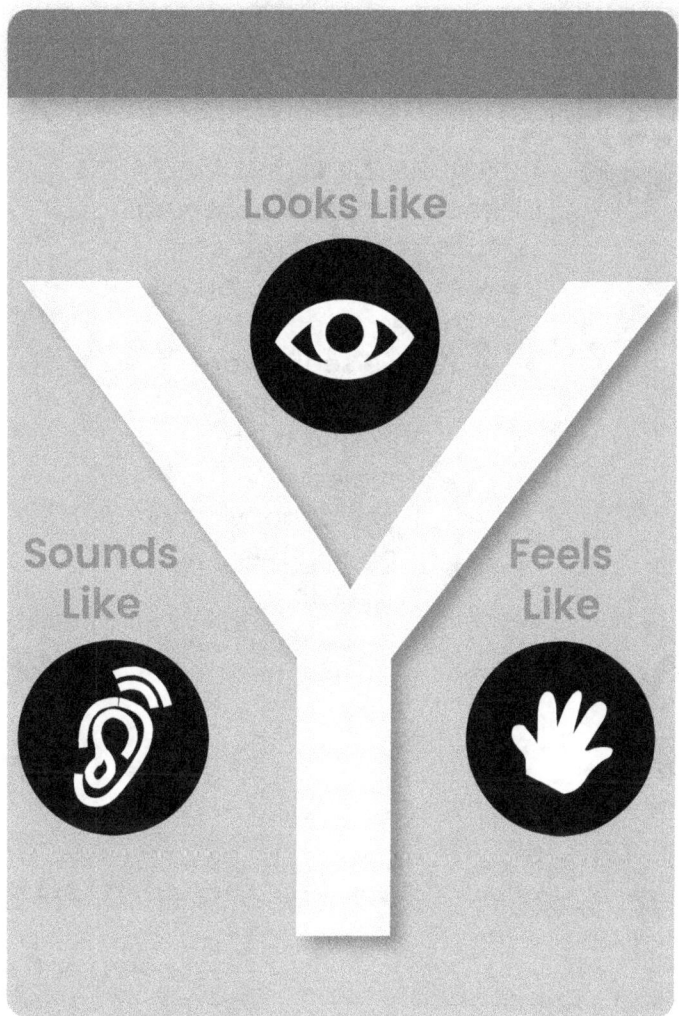

Description

The Y chart is a descriptive tool that can be used to write about what something looks like, feels likes and sounds like. The Y chart provides students with a visual framework in which to gather and write all their thoughts.

Scenario

You are stranded in the jungle. Record what you see, hear and feel in the jungle.

- Organise the class into working groups of three or four students.
- Provide each group with a large sheet of butcher's paper and coloured pens.

Once the students have recorded their ideas, it becomes a much easier task for them to write a letter or a diary account of their adventure. Key words have been identified and the range of ideas provides more stimuli for them.

Jungle Y Chart

Looks Like
- Monkeys, birds and lizards
- Green colours everywhere
- Lots of scary creatures
- Wet and damp ground
- Snakes, frogs, spiders
- Will we see Tarzan?
- Spooky and scary
- Dark and misty
- Tangled trees
- Huge canopy
- Torn clothes
- Cold

Sounds Like
- Raindrops falling
- Lots of growling sounds
- Eerie sounds
- Birds chirping
- Snakes hissing
- Owls hooting
- Lions growling
- Squealing monkeys
- Croaking frogs
- Slithering snakes
- Crawling insects
- Whistling wind
- Rustling noises
- Ground shaking

Feels Like
- Scared and frightened
- Insecure and worried
- Alone and dehydrated
- Wet and cold
- I'm hungry … Where is Mum?
- Mosquitoes biting you
- I need a shower
- Things brushing against you
- Tiny, tired, thirsty
- You're going to lose the plot
- Scary eyes watching me
- Angry, sad, lonely, crying
- I'm busting – I need a toilet!
- It's so hot – I'm suffocating.

Choosing the right Thinking Tool

Knowing the tools is important, but understanding when to use them is crucial. To give teachers practice in deciding which tools are best to use, choose one of the scenarios from the table below and select the best thinking tool to use in solving the problem. In some tasks, several tools may be used consecutively to solve a problem.

Activity	Thinking tool(s)
Write a rap song about your country.	
You have just returned from your school camp. On the camp you tried many different activities. Write a report about the various activities and how you felt about each of them.	
If you were Prime Minister, what would you change about your country?	
Write a "top five holiday destinations" list for each member of your family.	
You have been chosen for an Australian junior sporting team. How might other people feel about this?	
Design and carry out an experiment to find out whether plants need light.	
Design a new piece of jewellery. It should be original – it should be something that is new and different.	
The Education Department has decided that the only drink allowed in schools is water. No other drinks can be brought from home or sold in the tuck shop or canteen. What effect will this decision have?	
Write a report on the different varieties of dinosaurs that have been discovered. Show the locations of where each type of dinosaur was found.	
Create a diagram to show the structure of the Australian government.	
Write a one-page essay on a sport that you like.	
Describe the ecosystem of the rainforest.	
Design a new form of single person transport.	
Rewrite your own version of *The Three Little Pigs*.	
Every year the school has a billy cart race and as this is your last year at this school, you would really like to win. Make a plan of action to ensure that you achieve this goal.	

Activity	Thinking tool(s)
How good are you at completing homework? Evaluate your performance.	
Prepare a debate on euthanasia.	
What would happen if you tried to grow plants in a box with the top covered in green cellophane, with holes for air to circulate? Would this increase the growth of the plant? Why or why not?	
How can we effectively deal with bullying?	
Should there be separate gym classes for girls and boys?	
Use a diagram to explain the organisation of your school.	
Your parents are planning to move to another town and they have asked for your opinion. What will you tell them?	
Your local council has decided to allow a world-class theme park to be built in your neighbourhood. Write a report either for or against this proposal.	
Prepare a debate on whether animals should be used in experiments.	
Your school is going to be closed down. The nearest school is half an hour away. What effect will this have on you, the other students and your local area?	
You have decided to start a crocodile or llama farm. Prepare a report on what resources you will need and what you will need to know to start the farm.	
Read and summarise a report on human cloning.	
Compare the advantages of a holiday in Australia with a holiday in the United States of America.	
Your parents have given you permission to redecorate your room. Before they will allow you to go ahead, they want to discuss your plans and the costs involved. Make a plan of what changes you would like to make and calculate the costs.	
Invent a new and improved kind of hair dryer.	
Should human cloning be allowed? Prepare a speech.	

Action plan for implementation

You are now ready to commence developing your whole – school or faculty – based thinking skills program. The following steps have helped many schools to achieve this most worthwhile goal.

1. Receive support from the administrative team and teachers.

2. Establish a committee with the following aims:

    (a) Become familiar with the thinking tools that have been created by a number of educators and authors in the field.

    (b) Introduce these thinking tools to staff on a regular basis at staff meetings, etc.

3. Teachers implement these tools in their own classrooms to find out whether or not they work with their students.

4. Teachers continue to "experiment" with the implementation of these tools until they have selected a minimum of 25 thinking tools.

5. At this stage, each teacher is ready to finalise their own thinking toolkit containing a minimum of 25 thinking tools.

6. Develop your whole – school (primary) or faculty – based (secondary) thinking skills program.

7. Implement, review, monitor and adjust as necessary your thinking skills program on an annual basis.

Scenario

A Year 8 geography class made up of 28 students is studying global warming. The teacher wants the students to brainstorm all they know about global warming and asks the students to work with a partner. The class is divided up into 14 pairs of students. Once the teacher has revised TPS, each pair is given five minutes to compile a list of the ideas generated.

The teacher collects the lists and is disappointed with the quality of the responses received. Primarily, the students have provided responses such as:

> "Man causes global warming."
>
> "Cars pollute the air."
>
> "Flying is bad because it destroys the ozone layer."

TPS and TPSS

TPS (Think, pair, share) is a great cooperative learning strategy as it invites a group of two students to:

Think about the topic, issue or problem being investigated.

Pair with another student.

Share knowledge about the topic, issue or problem being investigated.

TPS can become difficult if one of the students is reluctant to engage in a conversation or if they have little knowledge or interest in the topic, issue or problem being discussed. This is where TPSS has proven to be useful. So how can we use TPSS?

TPSS stands for:

Think

Pair

Share

Square (meaning four students are now involved)

At this stage, the teacher decides to use TPSS and joins pairs of students, creating a total of seven groups of four students instead of the original 14 pairs. Each group is given five minutes to compile a new list of ideas. As the teacher moves around the room, it becomes clear that by using TPSS no group is dominated by just one student and the reluctant children have the opportunity to interact with the three other students in their group.

The teacher collects the new lists and notices:

- a marked improvement in the number of responses generated
- the new responses are deeper and broader than the original ones
- the new responses show that the students are becoming aware of the interacting factors that lead to global warming, such as:

    "We need to use more energy from the sun to manufacture goods because that creates less CO_2."

    "We should stop using coal to generate electricity because it generates a lot of CO_2."

    "Instead of travelling by car, we should be using trains and buses because they produce less pollution."

Reflection

- Based on the results received, in future should the teacher use only TPSS or is there some value in using TPS first?
- Once the new groups were created, the teacher asked the students to compile new lists. Should the teacher have asked the students to revise and improve the original lists that were generated by using TPS?
- Are there other thinking tools that should have been used by the teacher in this activity? If so, list them.
- Is five minutes enough time for students to brainstorm what they know about global warming?
- Do you have any suggestions for how to improve this activity?

The TPSS Method

1. Think
2. Pair
3. Share
4. Square

The author is grateful to Professor Frank Lyman for his permission to update TPS to TPSS.

References

Albert, M. (2004). *How the Birds Got Their Colours.* Australia: Scholastic.

Baker, J. (1987). *Where The Forest Meets The Sea.* London: Walker Books.

Bloom, B.S. (ed.) (1956). *Taxonomy of Educational Objectives. Book 1: Cognitive Domain.* New York: Longman.

Crowe, N. (2011). Private correspondence.

De Bono, E. (1976) *Teaching Thinking.* London: Penguin Group.

Gardner, H. (1999). *Intelligences Reframed, Multiple Intelligences for the 21st Century.* New York: Basic Books.

Hartnett, S. (2004). *The Silver Donkey.* Melbourne, Australia: Penguin Group.

Hince, V. (2011). Private correspondence.

Humphrey, A. (December 2005). 'SWOT Analysis for Management Consulting'. *SRI Alumni Association Newsletter.* Menlo Park, California: SRI International.

Lewis, C.I. (1918). *A Survey of Symbolic Logic.* Berkeley, California: University of California Press.

Lyman, F. (2007). Private correspondence.

Makepeace, M. (2011). Private correspondence.

Margulies, M.A. (1992) *Mapping Inner Space.* Melbourne, Victoria: Hawker Brownlow Education.

McGilvray, K. (2011). Private correspondence.

Pirozzo, R. (2006). *50 Cooperative Learning Activities.* Melbourne, Victoria: Hawker Brownlow Education.

Pirozzo, R. (2007). *Improving Thinking in the Classroom,* 2nd edn. Melbourne, Victoria: Hawker Brownlow Education.

Pirozzo, R. (2012). 'Differentiating and Personalising the Curriculum'. Conference held at Marist College, Ashgrove, Brisbane.

Stimson, J. (1996). *The Three Little Pigs.* London: Ladybird Books.

www.ingramcontent.com/pod-product-compliance
Lightning Source LLC
Chambersburg PA
CBHW081918090526

44590CB00019B/3396